In-Home Pet Euthanasia Techniques

The Veterinarian's Guide to Helping Pets and Their Families Say Goodbye in the Comfort of Home

Kathleen Cooney, D.V.M.

2nd Edition

In-Home Pet Euthanasia Techniques

Copyright © 2016 by Kathleen Cooney, D.V.M., MS

www.kathleencooneydvm.com

All Rights Reserved: No part of this publication may be reproduced, stored in a retrieval system or transmitted in any form or by any means, electronic, mechanical, photocopying, recording, scanning or otherwise, except as permitted under Sections 107 or 108 of the 1976 United States Copyright Act, without the prior written permission of the Publisher.

Limit of Liability/Disclaimer of Warranty: The publisher makes no representations or warranties with respect to the accuracy or completeness of the contents of this work and specifically disclaim all warranties, including without limitation warranties of fitness for a particular purpose. No warranty may be created or extended by sales or promotional materials. The advice and strategies contained herein may not be suitable for every situation. This work is sold with the understanding that the publisher is not engaged in rendering legal, accounting, or other professional services. If professional assistance is required, the services of a competent professional person should be sought. The publisher shall not be liable for damages arising herefrom.

All photos used in this publication were either purchased from iStockphoto.com or taken by the company Home to Heaven with expressed permission from the families.

The fact that an organization or Website is referred to in this work as a citation and/or a potential source of further information does not mean that the author endorses the information the organization or Website may provide or recommendations it may make.

Book design by White Space Graphics, LLC

www.whitespacegraphics.com

Table of Contents

Introduction 4
Chapter 1: **The Initial Discussion** 7
    The Decision to Euthanize 7
    Quality-of-Life Worksheet 11
    Describing the Process 13
    Aftercare Options 14
    Handling Payment 14
Chapter 2: **The Paperwork** 17
    Euthanasia Consents and Body Disposition Contracts 17
    Medication and Consultation Forms 19
    Sedation Permission Forms and Medication Release Forms 20
Chapter 3: **The Black Bag** 22
Chapter 4: **The Appointment** 27
    Making Preparations – Family 27
    Making Preparations – Doctor 32
    Setting the Stage 35
    Sedation/Anesthesia 39
    Catheter Placement 54
    Euthanasia Techniques 63
    Routes of Administration 70
    Time to Grieve 84
    Death: What to Expect 92
Chapter 5: **Paw Prints and Other Keepsakes** 98
Chapter 6: **Transportation for Cremation** 104
    Vehicle Arrangements 104
    Moving the Body 105
Chapter 7: **Aftercare: Cremation and Home Burial** 110
    Cremation 110
    Burial 111
    Disposal 117
Chapter 8: **Potential Problems** 119
    Aggressive Pets 119
    Personal Safety 123
Chapter 9: **Common Questions from Clients** 126
Chapter 10: Starting a Euthanasia Service 136
Conclusion 141
A Word from the Author 144
Appendices 145
References 150

Introduction

In-home pet euthanasia is nothing new. In fact, before treating companion animals in the clinic became the norm, most euthanasias were conducted at home. When fieldwork began giving way to clinic-based medicine, pets much more commonly spent their final moments in an exam room. Fortunately, many veterinarians recognized the importance of being at home during this significant time and kept in-home euthanasias from disappearing completely. Now with increased recognition of the human-animal bond, pet euthanasia is making its way back home, and this will undoubtedly become the norm again. Techniques are improving, and we are learning more about what families want and how to keep pets comfortable at home.

When I first came up with the idea for this book, it was meant to be an employee manual for my new doctors, to help them understand the differences between in-clinic and in-home euthanasia. During the writing process, however, it became clear to me that veterinarians nationwide could benefit from a comprehensive pet euthanasia-training manual. And so, over the course of the last 3 years, I have gathered together my experiences along with the teachings of some highly respected experts in pet loss, philosophy, and veterinary medicine.

The purpose of this book is to educate you about the many facets of in-home pet euthanasia and what, in most instances, makes it superior to euthanasias performed in the clinic. Whether you are new to veterinary medicine or a seasoned practitioner, I hope you learn what providing a peaceful in-home euthanasia experience involves. I will walk you through an appointment from beginning to end and address all the pertinent material one should know before starting out. I will also talk about how to handle those difficult situations that make many a veterinarian second guess whether they want to perform euthanasias in the home. When you have finished reading, you will have expanded your understanding of sedation protocols, euthanasia techniques, pet loss support, how to exceed client expectations, and much more.

Why do so many families choose in-home euthanasia for their pets? Simply stated, it is the comfort that only home can provide anyone facing death and the loss of a loved one. No one ever says they want to spend their final moments in a hospital. They want to be at home surrounded by loved ones and whenever possible, pets deserve the same level of compassion. What an in-home euthanasia provider can offer is priceless during a pet's final hour. You know what to expect in any situation, you can anticipate the family's needs, and portray the compassion, confidence, and control they rely on.

This is a time of great evolution and momentum within geriatric medicine, pet hospice, and pet euthanasia. As pets become more adored as family members and surrogate children, their entire lives will be handled with the utmost care and respect, and this includes the time around their deaths. As with any new leap forward, lasting change will take time. The availability of pet hospice and euthanasia services is on the rise across the country and can only enhance the public's appreciation of in-home care. By working together, we have the opportunity to improve the level of care a pet receives from the time it develops a terminal condition to the moment the family says goodbye, through either a natural death or euthanasia. In fact, this time of disease for the pet and the anticipatory grief felt by the family is what needs the greatest attention. Too often we are called upon to euthanize a pet that has been suffering for days or even months with little to no attention paid to the management of its basic needs. By reaching out to families early, we can offer guidance and help make the death of a pet a smoother transition for everyone involved.

I hope this material spurs discussion among practitioners and encourages you to learn as much as you can about end-of-life care. Over the next few years, continuing education opportunities touching on topics like pain management in the dying pet, compassion fatigue, and euthanasia techniques should be easier to find than they are now. I encourage you to reach out to your fellow in-home euthanasia providers to create friendships and learn what is working for them, on both a technical and personal level.

"A house is not a home without a pet."

~ Anonymous

Chapter 1

The Initial Discussion

The Decision to Euthanize

The decision to euthanize a beloved pet is one of the hardest issues anyone has to face. It is often wrapped in various emotions such as guilt, uncertainty, confusion, fear, and overwhelming sadness. When a family is confronted with a pet's terminal illness, these emotions often guide their decision making process. The veterinarian's role is to listen, offer expertise and understanding, and above all else, be non-judgmental but always supportive for the pet's cause.

The questions I hear from clients time and time again are:

- How will I know it is the right time?
- Why doesn't she just pass peacefully in the night?
- What are the signs that she is suffering?
- Will she tell me when she's ready?

Our experience as veterinarians tells us that the answers to these questions are very complicated and almost entirely depend on the individual pet in question. Specializing in a euthanasia-centered practice, I see the internal struggle families have with anticipatory grief and trying to do what is best. What they seem to question the most is whether or not their pet is in pain and what signs they should look for that indicate suffering. We can help guide families regarding what symptoms indicate that death is coming and give recommendations for managing pain and the pet's basic needs, but the decision of when to say goodbye is ultimately theirs. If a family wants me to tell them to euthanize, and I feel that it is in the pet's best interest, I am honest and give my blessing.

If you provide this service long enough, you will face a family's request to euthanize a pet that you feel still has a good quality of life. Animals tend to hide their illness, and the family may be seeing more physical signs of deterioration than you might observe at first. This is a delicate situation and one where all sides of the story need to be heard. Good client communication goes a long way towards understanding what the family needs and what they are really trying to say to you. I try to reserve judgment regarding euthanasia until I've heard the full story. The owner has worked up a lot of courage to call me and getting all of the details is necessary to make a sound decision regarding the pet's future.

> *A woman called me one time to say her dog needed to be put down because he had cancer. He had just been diagnosed with lymphoma, and with no treatment, had been given 4 weeks or so to live. She and her family decided they would not treat and in fact, had decided to proceed with euthanasia now rather than wait until they saw signs of suffering. The family had made this decision because this was their fourth dog with lymphoma and they knew the path it would take if they waited much longer. I agreed to help them, and when I arrived at the house, the dog greeted me at the door wagging his tail with a ball in his mouth. When I saw him and the look on everyone's faces, I knew this was the right thing to do. There is a popular saying in veterinary medicine "I would rather help my friend a month too early than an hour too late." This family had seen what an hour too late looks like and wanted to spare their dog from it. I've seen many 'hour too late' situations, and if this family was willing to let their pet go while he was still happy, I was OK with that.*

Granted, veterinarians are often asked to euthanize pets that are not sick at all, and communication is the key to deciphering what is truly going on. If it is a clear case of convenience, like moving into a house that doesn't take pets, euthanasia is not the answer. When we find ourselves in the home ready to euthanize, it doesn't mean we have to continue if we have been mislead about the pet's status. Let your instinct, life experience, and education guide you toward the best course of action for everyone.

Families need to understand that euthanasia is a personal choice. There is no rule or law stating that an owner must euthanize a pet under any circumstance. If the pet is suffering, either physically or mentally, the family ultimately has the right to decide how they want to proceed. Other options, such as hospice care, do exist and can be utilized up until a natural death occurs. The important thing is that the family is helped in making some sort of decision to aid their pet rather than letting nature simply "take its course." When hospice care or euthanasia is available, choosing to do nothing is making the choice to let the pet suffer. I have never had a family tell me they chose euthanasia too soon. It is almost always "We waited too long."

I often talk to families about death as a natural event in nature. If we look at an old rottweiler that has been unable to stand for weeks, we know that he is still with us due to our intervention. If he were in the wild, or even just in the backyard without help, nature would have taken its course. Starvation, predation, and the elements would have led to a quicker death. When we bring pets into the home and provide them with food, shelter, and medical care, death is likely to take longer and has the potential to become more complicated. It is wonderful that we can provide for animals, but in doing so I think we also take on the responsibility of saying when "enough is enough." As Dr. Bernard Rollin so eloquently teaches, it is our responsibility to provide for our animals, both in life and in death. It is our unwritten contract with animals that says once we have established a bond, and have agreed to partner in life with them, we will meet their needs, both mentally and physically. When end-of-life is upon them, it is our responsibility to ensure they do not suffer. If an animal's pain cannot be managed and the basic functions of life are threatened, euthanasia's "good death" can be our greatest gift.

For most, euthanasia is an acceptable choice for many reasons:

- End the pain and suffering
- Guarantee a peaceful death
- Allow family members and friends to be present
- Maintain the human-animal bond

When families choose euthanasia, usually their wish is to end the suffering they see their pet enduring. My favorite definition of suffering is, in its purist form, "anything that denies us our true self." For our animals, this can be obvious physical pain or mental pain, for instance the inability to engage in the activities that bring them joy. None of us want our pets to suffer. Therefore, euthanasia can be a real blessing. Almost daily, I hear from families how we are kinder to our pets that are suffering than our own human family members faced with debilitating illness. I like to remind my clients that the only way to end their pet's suffering is to make their own begin. It is meant to be a very difficult decision.

In-Home Pet Euthanasia Techniques

Euthanasia's goal is a peaceful death. So many of us hope for the morning when we wake up and find that our pet has made the difficult decision for us and passed quietly in the night, but this is unfortunately a relatively rare occurrence. And the question remains if they die in the night, how do we know it's peaceful? Did they struggle for air? Were there any seizures or painful moments? Frankly, we just don't know. Choosing to euthanize helps ensure that death will come quickly and that the end of life is as pain free as possible.

Another reason to choose euthanasia is to allow family and friends to gather with the pet. Simply put, death is a part of life, and it is an honor to have loved ones gathered around paying tribute and mourning the loss of their friend. People often share with me the sadness they felt when they couldn't be present for the death of another pet. They feel guilty that they didn't stay for euthanasia in the vet's office or are fearful that their pet died a horrible death while they were sleeping. The unknowns haunt them. If we have come to the conclusion that euthanasia is the best answer for a beloved pet, then choosing a time to achieve it is the next step. This is incredibly hard for families and should be approached delicately and with great respect.

It may seem strange to some to think of euthanasia as honoring the human-animal bond, but when chosen with the right intentions, it couldn't be truer. When a family chooses euthanasia, they have found the strength to put their sadness aside and focus on what the pet needs. Except in the cases of convenience euthanasia, it is a very unselfish act, one made out of love.

> *I recently received a call from an old rancher who wanted his dog put down. The dog had cancer and was getting sicker and sicker. He knew her spirit was broken. He called me because she'd been his working dog all her life. She was there for him during his hip surgery, through his divorce, and now she needed him like never before. He wanted to honor the bond between them and give her the peace she so desperately needed. This rancher told me he was too weak himself to lift her anymore and carry her outside for potty breaks. He was sharing his guilt over his physical limitations, and I could tell he felt that he had already waited too long to do something*

for her. As I was listening to him, I kept thinking how lucky this dog was that her owner loved her enough to take on such sadness to help her. Here he was putting aside his needs to end her suffering.

What if the family doesn't want euthanasia and pain and suffering is present? Many people do not believe in ending life before nature runs its course. Devout Buddhists believe that pain and/or suffering is a rite of passage for humans and something that cleanses the soul before death. After talking with some Buddhist clients, they have shared with me that pets don't have to go through this cleansing. Whatever the belief, legally a pet is personal property, and the owner has the right to proceed with end-of-life issues as they see fit as long as adequate veterinary care is provided. When euthanasia is not an option, it is our ethical responsibility as veterinarians to educate owners on how to treat their pet's condition as best they can. If you are unable to provide the necessary services, you can always refer to another veterinarian who can.

Hospice care for pets is rapidly advancing and becoming more widely available. Human hospice, developed by nurses attending to dying patients, is a long-standing practice, and with the maturation of the human-animal bond, it is a natural movement forward in veterinary medicine. Hospice care can be used to keep a pet comfortable before euthanasia and for the pet whose family prefers a natural death. It is a very broad topic and beyond the scope of this book, but if you know a family is really struggling with the decision to euthanize, make sure they understand their options for in-home hospice care. Help them recognize the full extent of their pet's disease, what to expect as death approaches, and provide information about palliative treatments that can keep their pet as comfortable as possible. Also, make sure they realize that even with all that medicine has to offer, both conventional and holistic forms, they might still get to the point where the impending death is difficult for everyone. Help them to evaluate what the pet would want.

Quality-of-Life Worksheet

Entire books have been written about quality-of-life as it pertains to veterinary patients. For our purposes, we will talk about factors that we can use to assess quality of life, from both the pet and client's point of view.

Over the years, veterinarians and animal lovers have devised many quality of-life grading scales to make it easier for families to ascertain when euthanasia might be appropriate. The scales include physical and mental factors that can be scored and tallied up to determine whether or not life remains bearable for the pet. Dr. Alice Villalobos, in her book *Canine and Feline Geriatric Oncology: Honoring the Human-Animal Bond*, has just such a scale. Hers is designed to open up discussion among family members about what their pet needs to continue a pleasant, fulfilling life. Scales like this aim to be objective during an overwhelming emotional time. They can be used to evaluate the success of hospice care and/or look at the health and happiness of a pet that is not receiving medical care.

Factors assessed in quality-of-life scales include:

- Appetite
- Hydration
- Hygiene
- Pain
- Mobility
- Mental status
- Happiness
- Good days versus bad days
- Urination
- Defecation

Every scale is a little different from the next, but the goal of them all is to help the family and veterinarian understand what is happening with the pet and proceed with the best course of action (e.g., improve pain control, offer better nutrition, manage pressure sores, etc.). Quality-of-life scales can be the "reality check" that helps a family come to the decision to euthanize. If the family is not yet ready, then together you can decide how best to proceed. Please see the Quality of Life PDF included in your purchased ebook folder.

I also find it helpful for families to make a list of things their pet enjoys doing. This list, like the scale, can be a fallback when emotions are running high and anticipatory grief is taking over. I remember when my husband and I were faced with managing our elderly lab's health. He had arthritis, panted all the time, and stumbled quite a bit. Early in his fourteenth year,

I found a primary lung tumor, which appeared to be slow growing. My husband didn't want to talk much about it, so I suggested we make a list of the things that McKenzie enjoyed. He liked to sleep at night in our bedroom downstairs, he loved meeting new dogs at the park, and he never missed an opportunity to eat. We decided that when he could no longer get down the five steps to our basement, cross the yard to say hi to a passing dog, breathe easily, or seek out food, then we would talk about euthanasia. A few months after we made the list, he started falling down the steps. He started having stress diarrhea in the house because it was too hard for him to navigate even the one step into the back yard. We helped him as best we could, but soon saw how much his efforts were taking out of him. We even stopped taking him to the park. He never did lose his appetite or struggle to breathe, but the rest of his troubles were enough and we let him go. The list we made for him was our guide and it forced us to acknowledge the changes we were seeing.

In summary, veterinarians have a very important role in the lives of our clients facing the loss of a pet and in the life of the pet itself. We must listen to their story, determine what course of action will be best suited for everyone, remain non-judgmental and supportive when appropriate, and always have compassion toward the situation.

Describing the Process

When an owner is ready to talk about euthanasia, remember that you are describing the final moments they will ever have with their beloved pet. It doesn't matter if you've talked about it with six other people that day; this is a unique conversation for them. Speak slowly and softly, focusing all of your attention on them. It may have taken months for this person to gather the strength to reach out for help.

When I speak to a client for the first time, I try to let them do most of the talking at the beginning. They can share with me information about the pet's disease, factors that are influencing their decision, and when they might want to have me come to their home. When they are ready, I go over what will take place during an appointment. We talk about sitting down for a few minutes to go over the paperwork and make sure that we have everything in order for the pet's aftercare. Next we talk about any preparations that need to be made, like when and where to gather, who will be there, etc. I tell them about the sedation their pet will receive to keep them sleeping throughout the euthanasia. Families don't need much detail about sedation, just the reassurance that their pets will be comfortable. When it comes to the euthanasia itself, I simply state that I will proceed when the pet and the family is ready. We talk about the paw print I can make for them, and then I ask what they have decided for the pet's aftercare. I go into these details so that clients know what to expect, but often much of what I have said is forgotten. When in grief, families have a huge need to be understood, but have little capacity to understand. Be prepared to go over everything again during the appointment.

All of this can be done over the phone or during an in-home consultation. If the family is unsure about euthanasia, set up an in-home meeting with family members so you can talk about their concerns, perform a physical exam, and describe the euthanasia process in more detail. Some people need to know every detail about what their pet's death will involve, and you will have time to oblige them during the in-home consultation. Phone conversations lack the personal connection that you get with a face-to-face meeting.

Aftercare Options

During the initial discussion, it is appropriate to talk about aftercare arrangements like cremation, body donation, or burial. Sometimes families focus so much on the loss of their pet that they overlook how they will manage the body after death. Open up a dialog on the subject as the preparations for euthanasia take place. One family member may want cremation while another one would like burial. Having details like this discussed ahead of time eliminates stress during your appointment. More details about specific types of aftercare can be found in Chapter Seven.

Handling Payment

Veterinarians are notoriously reluctant to discuss fees, but it is a topic that should be touched upon early in your conversation. Some people call and want to know prices right away. Others will ask once everything else has been discussed. Sometimes you will have to bring up the subject yourself. Whenever the topic does come up, keep everything simple

and straightforward. Determine what the total fee will be during your conversation, including charges for cremation, so there are no surprises later on. Make sure clients know about any emergency fees you might have for an after-hours appointment. Do not put yourself in a position where you have to explain extra charges when you arrive at the family's home.

I have had many clients sound guilty when they ask how much everything is going to cost. Quite often, families spend thousands of dollars on diagnostics and treatments only to find that they do not have money left over for a peaceful passing at home like they really want. When talking about the price of your services to prospective clients, let them see the value in what you offer. Help them understand the beauty of what you are providing for their pet in the comfort of home. If a client's finances are tight, consider setting up a payment plan or other arrangements. Being flexible builds trust and support of your work in the community. My service accepts cash, check, VISA, and MasterCard. Accepting credit cards helps families caught up in an emergency and those who are unprepared for the cost of veterinary services.

If you are collecting payment during the appointment, try to get it out of the way before moving forward with euthanasia. Once the pet has died, family members are distraught and need to focus on their own grief and needs. I might kindly say "Would you like to take care of financial things now or before I leave?" Most people want to take care of payment up front and then focus the remaining time on their pet. In an emergency situation, however, collect payment at the end of the appointment so that you can focus on the pet's needs first. If it feels especially awkward to ask for payment, I might inform a client that I will send an invoice later in the week, and they can take care of it when they are ready.

Having payment prepared before the appointment is ideal. Clients can have a check written out for the total amount and then just hand it to you when the time is right. With credit cards, you can take the necessary information over the phone so that fees are not even discussed during the appointment. We call these prepayments, and they really work nicely.

"I love cats because I enjoy my home; and little by little, they become its visible soul."

~ Jean Cocteau

Chapter 2

The Paperwork

Whenever I enter the home, I have all of my necessary forms and material with me. As part of the preparation time, I ready my binder that carries everything I need: consent forms, fee sheets, credit card slips, identification cards for the crematories, and grief support material. Everything is neatly organized and easy to find. Being thoroughly prepared helps to build client confidence in me and allows for a smooth beginning to the appointment.

Euthanasia Consents and Body Disposition Contracts

Paperwork is something most of us like to avoid, but there are times when it is necessary. A good consent form or contract will provide you with important information; it will help the client to focus on what is happening; and when signed, protect you the veterinarian from certain legal repercussions. The contract can also serve as your medical record by including the owner's and animal's information, medical history, etc. Once you have a good contract, with spaces for all the information you need, make sure it is filled out to completion during or shortly after every appointment. It will save you headaches down the road.

My service uses one form that serves as the contract for services, medical record, body disposition request, and drug log. During the appointment, the veterinarian sits down with the family and gently discusses its content. It is helpful to have everything filled in as much as possible before the appointment. Then all you have to do is verify the information with the family, such as the spelling of names. With new clients, this is also a nice time to ask how they heard of your service. If you have room on your contract, leave a space where you can write down this referral source. You can then go back and thank your referrals later.

For legal purposes, have a lawyer review your contract. They will ensure that everything you need to protect yourself is included. Our contract makes three important legal statements that the client has to sign off on. The first is that the pet in question is theirs and/or they have complete authority to request euthanasia. The second is that they agree to all the terms of our services and that all of the information on the form is correct. The third legal statement pertains to rabies exposure. The family needs to certify that the pet has not exposed anyone to rabies within the last 10 days. When presenting this to the family, I try to soften the wording by saying something like "This statement here just says that Ruby has not exposed anyone to rabies in the last 10 days, which seems most unlikely, but I just want you to know what you are signing."

As can only be expected, most of the people preparing to say goodbye to their beloved pets are distraught and not thinking clearly. Help them through the form and make sure they understand everything that they are agreeing to. Keep the form easy to read, free of unnecessary jargon, and if possible, limited to one side of a sheet of paper so nothing gets missed. After going over the form, have them sign and date it. If you suspect that your client has been drinking or is under the influence of drugs, make sure to get multiple signatures on the consent form to protect yourself and the company you are working for.

If your policy is to notify all treating veterinarians of the euthanasias that you perform, leave space on the contract for clinic names. You can ask the family who has treated the pet in the last three to five years and notify the clinics for them. This will help eliminate inappropriate vaccine reminders and uncomfortable calls from vets checking to see how the pet is doing. In my experience, this is a huge referral builder with local vet clinics. They like knowing that when they refer to us, we will notify them via fax within 24 hours of the euthanasia.

Include space on your contract for the pet's signalment and presenting condition. We include the name, sex, breed, age, weight, and presenting condition, which can be as simple as stating "age related changes" or more detailed like "osteoarthritis, weight loss, cataracts, deafness, and dementia." Mention anything that a referring vet might need to know as to why the pet was euthanized as well as what will help you remember the case down the road. In my experience, writing down "osteosarcoma" is not as memorable as "osteosarcoma of the left stifle." A bit more detail helps me remember the patient, especially when I call the family to see how they are doing or they phone me needing help with another pet.

Kathleen Cooney, D.V.M.

If you will be making arrangements for the pet's aftercare, add a section on the form for body disposition details. Include where you will be taking the pet and what service will be performed. In the case of private cremation, arrangements need to be made to get the ashes back to the family. Will they be going to the crematory themselves or will you be bringing the ashes to them? Many crematories will deliver ashes to local veterinary clinics or to the family's home at no additional charge. Going over this information before the euthanasia is very helpful. Some people can barely speak afterwards, and you will have a hard time easily working it into the conversation.

Save room at the bottom of your form for "office use only." The last 1/5 of our form contains a drug log, doctor's signature, and records of payment collected. We refer back to it for accounting purposes and drug recording. Keep your contracts on file for at least 5 years; they are legal documents. If possible, just file them away somewhere in case you need to look something up later on.

Medication and Consultation Forms

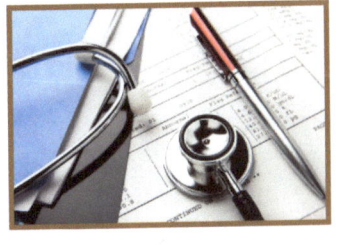

For the purpose of good record keeping, you should have a way to keep track of all non-euthanasia work that you do. My service has color-coordinated forms that are easy to locate among our mass of binders. Our consultation-only forms contain the family's information, the pet's signalment and history, and the vet's plan for medical care. We have a section for a follow up call and documentation of any changes that the pet is experiencing as the time for euthanasia approaches. Our policy is to call the family within seven days of our consultation to check in and to see if they are in need of guidance. Our medication forms contain the same client and patient information along with the medication instructions. When a client calls to request a refill, we can just refer back to the form and get them what they need. Many euthanasia services do not sell medications, but we have found that having a few special ones on hand makes things easier for the clients. We sell only the basics like pain medications, antibiotics, and joint supplements.

Many of our clients do not have a current relationship with a veterinarian before contacting us. If we can make the pet more comfortable until the family decides the time is right for euthanasia, that is what we do. If a pet needs subcutaneous fluid therapy, we keep extra bags, lines, and needles on hand to leave with the owner and instruct them on administration techniques. For anything more invasive than rehydration, pain management, and infection control, we refer to local clinics. More aggressive treatments might include palliative surgical procedures, feeding tube placement, etc.

Sedation Permission Forms and Medication Release Forms

There are times you will be called to the home to determine if euthanasia is the best course of action. If the pet is in pain and/or uncooperative, you may need to give a sedative first to perform a thorough physical exam to understand the pet's condition. If the family is hoping you find a treatable condition, make sure they understand the risk of sedation. Choose a sedative that can be reversed if the pet shows signs of distress. Have them sign a sedation release form in case the sedative leads to an untimely death.

Medication release forms are also important. If we sell an anti-inflammatory drug like Rimadyl®, clients sign a release stating they understand the risk of liver and kidney disease, gastric ulcers, etc. and that blood work is always recommended, but not required by us. Most of my patients are elderly and physically compromised, and giving medications might worsen a condition other than the one we are treating. Make sure families know the side effects and risks of any drug you prescribe. Our limited service does not perform blood testing so families are instructed to find a clinic that can. We keep these forms on file for five years, just like our euthanasia consent forms.

"Every boy should have two things: a dog, and a mother willing to let him have one."

~ Anonymous

In-Home Pet Euthanasia Techniques

Chapter 3

The Black Bag

For any mobile veterinarian, preparation is extremely important. All necessary supplies need to be on hand. There is no running back to the clinic when a family is waiting for a euthanasia. A good setup can make the difference between a successful appointment and a disastrous one.

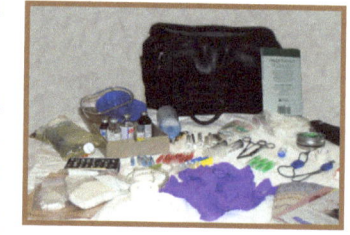

The black bag I use is the same one I've had for over three years. Its leather material is very durable, the interior is spacious, and it is easy to clean. Many dogs have licked it, drooled on it, and yes, peed on it, and it still looks great. Appearance counts. Your bag represents your professionalism, and families will judge your service based on first impressions. Your bag and your general appearance need to look trustworthy.

The contents of your bag need to be dependable too. Below is a detailed list of items you might consider bringing to an appointment.

- Bandage scissors
- White tape – 1 inch
- Hemostats
- Gauze 4x4s – soaked in hydrogen peroxide
- Calculator
- Pens
- Spinal needles (2)
- Rubber gloves
- Grief books
- Skin adhesive
- Clay paw print kits
- Cordless clippers with 40-blade
- Letter stamping kit for paw prints
- Tourniquets – small nylon (2)
- Tupperware container for trash
- Catheters – 22 and 24 gauge
- Sterile saline solution
- Needles – 1 inch 18, 22, and 25 gauge 1.5 inch 18 and 22 gauge
- Drug box, drugs, and key
- Prescription pad
- Syringes – 1 ml, 3 ml, 6 ml, 12 ml, 20 ml
- Brochures – for your service, crematories, etc.
- Male adapters – short luer lock
- Pepper spray
- Extension sets – 3 ml capacity
- Band-Aids®
- Stethoscope
- Kleenex®
- Flashlight
- Business cards

Every item probably won't be used during every appointment, but they all have their time and place. For example, the bandage scissors come in handy when you need to remove a well-secured catheter that was left in by a referring vet. The skin adhesive can be used to close the eyelids of pets remaining at home for burial. The rubber gloves are indispensable when trying to move a dog whose bowels have released or for any other messy job. The only medical items in my bag that I have never used are the spinal needles. I have them in case I need to perform a cardiac injection in a very large dog, but so far the 1.5-inch needles have worked just fine. As with many things in life, you only miss something once it's gone, so keep your bag well supplied.

Your bag should be fully outfitted to handle your planned methods of euthanasia. Most of my euthanasias are done intravenously, so catheters, tourniquets, adapters, white tape, needles, syringes, and saline are very important. I use 24 gauge catheters for pets under 30 pounds and 22 gauge catheters for larger pets. Try to stock at least 10 of each in case you have a hard time finding a vein. My bag is stocked with needles and syringes for administering sedatives, saline flush, or euthanasia solution. The 25 gauge needles are for intramuscular or subcutaneous sedative injections to help minimize discomfort. Some of my colleagues use 27 gauge or insulin needles. The widest needle, the 18 gauge, is for drawing up and administering euthanasia solution. Most pentobarbital drugs are highly viscous, and larger bore needles help to speed administration and cut down on the amount of pressure needed to express drugs. I also keep 1.5 inch 18 gauge needles for intracardiac and intrahepatic injections in big dogs. The shorter 1 inch size is good for intravenous and most intraabdominal injections. It is grueling trying to push large amounts of euthanasia solution through a long thin 22 gauge needle. The wider bore 18 gauge makes everything easier, and an anesthetized pet will not feel the difference. Stock syringes to fit your needs too. Mine range in size from 1 ml to 20 ml.

The saline solution takes up a fair amount of room in the bag. I carry a full liter with me in case the appointment changes from euthanasia to a consultation with palliative subcutaneous fluid therapy. Smaller bags or bottles are available if space in your bag is at a premium.

One-person catheter placement is challenging, so make it as easy as possible by using quality tools. In-home euthanasias sometimes occur in unexpected locations. You may gather with your patient under a pine tree on the edge of the property or in the back of a pickup with no electricity.

Quality cordless, rechargeable clippers are a must. Make sure your clippers are fully charged and ready to go. I use a 40 blade for a clean cut and better vein visibility. This being said, clipping is not required for catheter placement, but I have found that it saves me time and money on wasted catheters because I can see the vein well. Families are usually happier when catheter placement is quick and clipping the hair helps speed the process. My clipper brand of choice is Andis®.

A quality tourniquet is also a necessity when no one is available to help you hold off the vein. My service sends only doctors to the home, no technicians. We only ask a family member to assist us if the pet's skin is very loose and difficult to work with. The small nylon tourniquets we use are easy to store in the bag and actually hold up quite well. They eventually fray and need to be replaced, but some of mine have lasted six months or more. They are inexpensive, easy to replace, and sold in packs of two. Always carry two with you in case one breaks.

Other items used for intravenous euthanasia are male adapters and extension sets. I use male adapters to cap off the catheters much more frequently than extension sets. Our service helps a lot of big dogs and we like to place the catheter in the lateral saphenous of a hind leg. This keeps us away from the dog's head and allows the family to gather around their beloved pet. I use luer lock male adapters to keep the catheter setup tight. A leak can be very scary when you can't immediately determine it's origin and if you still have venous access. Take the guesswork out of the equation by using a luer lock and secure it tightly.

I use extension sets for those times that I want to sit back and give the family ample room to gather around their pet, as is usually the case with cats and small dogs. Many owners like to hold smaller pets on their laps. Once the catheter and extension set are secured, I can move away and administer the euthanasia solution as unobtrusively as possible. Some vets always use an extension set, regardless of the catheter position, to help shield owners from the more technical aspects of euthanasia. This is your choice. I have found that as long as you give the family room to breathe and be with their companion, they will be happy.

Gauze lightly soaked in hydrogen peroxide is a useful too. I keep a sandwich bag full of 4x4 gauze in my bag at all times. You can use them to clean up drops of blood, for instance at your catheter site once euthanasia is complete, and to clean your hands before molding clay for a paw print. I also keep a few Band-Aids® on hand in case I poke my finger with a needle.

Some of the bulkier items in the bag are the pet loss books, brochures, and bags containing clay for the memorial paw prints. If you find yourself performing multiple euthanasias per day, keep plenty of paw prints or other keepsakes of your choosing on hand. They are a nice way to help families remember their loved one and give them something to look upon for comfort. My full service includes one paw print, although every so often a family will want more. If your bag is big enough, you should be able to carry quite a few bags, each containing enough clay to make one print. I try to start the day prepared to help four families and stock my bag accordingly. My doctors each carry a letter stamping kit to add the pet's name and years of life to the paw print if the owner wishes. For information on where to obtain clay kits, letter stamps, and pet loss books, see the appendices at the end of the book.

Of course, you will need access to drugs during your euthanasia appointment. I recommend using a lock box of some sort, similar to a small cashbox, that can hold all of your bottles. Carrying multiple drugs makes your bag a target for theft, so be careful and keep things secure. My drug box requires a key to open, which prevents someone from just reaching in and helping themselves. The drugs that you need will be specific to your euthanasia protocol. My drug box contains xylazine, butorphanol or nalbuphine, Telazol®, acepromazine, Yohimbine®, and pentobarbital solution. If you can, keep 2 bottles of your euthanasia solution with you at all times. Too many vets have fallen victim to running out of solution during a euthanasia. If you see many appointments per day, it's easy to underestimate how much you may need. If you keep prescription pads with you, they also need to remain locked up.

What you bring into an appointment, you will need to take back out, and that includes your trash. Medical procedures mean medical waste and leaving behind any medical waste is a major no-no. Carry a small Tupperware® container in your bag to hold trash. This will help keep your bag clean and organized and ensures nothing is left behind for the family to discover later. By the end of the euthanasia, it may hold clipped hair, a catheter sheath and stylet, a few needles and syringes, used tape, and gauze.

"If you have to kill an animal, do it quickly and with skill so that the animal suffers as little as possible. Do well everything you do."

~ Muhammad

Chapter 4

The Appointment

Making Preparations – Family

Once the decision to euthanize has been made, the family of the pet in question will need to make preparations and decide how they would like to say goodbye. These preparations are very specific to each family and will reflect upon different factors, such as previous experiences, the comfort of the pet, time of day, etc. Providing the service at home opens up a whole host of possibilities. Most of the time, the family will have an idea of how they would like the euthanasia to take place by the time they make the initial call. If they don't, they might ask for guidance.

When preparing for in-home euthanasia, there are four factors to consider: who, what, where, and when. In a clinical setting, these factors are usually fairly rigid. Families often choose to say goodbye to their companions at home because of the extra flexibility it offers.

Who

Who wants to be present? Immediate family only or will close friends be invited too? How about other pets? For some owners, these questions will be very easy to answer while others might need weeks to prepare everyone and get schedules in order. Many euthanasias take place around the holidays when the family is all together. Some of my most memorable appointments have been when an entire family is together, sometimes as many as 20 people.

> *I was called out to help an old German shepherd named Duke, and when I got to the home, the driveway was full of cars. I can often tell which house on the street I'm going to because of all the cars parked in front, but this was beyond my wildest expectations. The only spot left for me was way out by the barn. You could hear chatter and laughter coming from the front door. Duke was lying in the sun-filled entryway, where he always liked to be. It gave him the best view of the*

In-Home Pet Euthanasia Techniques

house and yard. I was guided past Duke into the living room where the entire family had gathered, a total of about 20 or so. The grandparents and aunts and uncles were there as was the immediate family including a number of young children. This was to be a real sendoff for Duke, and no one wanted to miss it.

When it came time to be with their sweet old dog, I found myself stuck in the corner of the entry, between Duke and the wall, with not an inch to spare. I squeezed my bag in next to me and hoped that the catheter would place easily so no one would have to move. Duke was very big and didn't want to move from his favorite spot. Everyone gathered around as I explained how I would help him. There were lots of nods and eventually tears when I gave him the sedative. Then one of the uncles stepped forward and offered to read a prayer for Duke. The room quieted down, even the kids stood still for a few minutes while this man read his prayer. The family held hands while I proceeded to help Duke die with dignity, surrounded by his loved ones. One of the young children managed to work his way through the room to me. He crawled up onto my bag and watched me as I gently took Duke's paw in hand to make the paw print keepsake.

When it came time to leave, everyone wanted to help carry Duke out, to be one of his pallbearers. We all made our way out to the van and gently placed Duke's body inside. I turned around to say my goodbyes and there was the entire family, standing by for their hugs. I was blessed with more hugs that day than most people get in a month. Duke was a lucky dog and so was I to have shared this time with him and his family.

"Should the kids be there?" Some people have very strong opinions about this, both for and against. Parents are in the best position to decide, but they may need some guidance from you. The biggest concerns are whether or not the child will be emotionally traumatized from watching their pet die or harbor a lasting resentment toward the parents. From what I have seen over the years, kids do remarkably well when allowed to be present. Some will cry, some will tell funny stories, and some will be interested in the technical aspect of the euthanasia itself. If at all possible, I recommend that parents include children in decision-making and let them decide for themselves if they want to be present.

Should other family pets be present? This is a question I also hear again and again. As with children, pets do very well witnessing the euthanasia of their housemate. I have never seen any detrimental effects from a pet witnessing another pet's passing. In
fact, I would say just the opposite. Granted, the vast majority of pets show little understanding, at least from our perspective. They are usually more interested in the stranger in their home and all of the smells that you carry. However, there are those special few that seem to say "I know why you are here, and I am very concerned about my friend and family." Dogs can form very strong pack connections and openly grieve when a member is lost. If they understand that their friend is dying before them, some may even vocalize or come over to smell the body.

An important thing to keep in mind about having other pets present is that sometimes they want all of the attention for themselves. It can be hard for the family to spend quality time with their dying pet when another, rambunctious one is running around, crawling onto their laps, and throwing toys in the air. In these situations, I usually recommend putting the other pet outside until after the euthanasia is complete. Then they can come back in and be included. If the family really wants them there to witness the death, give the energetic pet a chance to settle down before proceeding. Other pets will often pick on their owner's anxieties and become nervous as a result. Help calm them with gentle words and tender touches. It is not uncommon for other pets to stay close to me since I am the calmest person in the room.

What

The 'what' in question is, of course, euthanasia itself. Ninety nine percent of the people you talk to will know what euthanasia means, but there will be that one percent who does not and this can lead to some interesting conversations. I had one young lady call me to see if my euthanasia service offered chinchilla house sitting. Needless to say, euthanasia is final, and everyone needs to be clear about what is taking place.

Where

The in-home euthanasia setting allows for various "where" scenarios, which is very appealing to families. This decision I like to leave almost entirely up to the family. The only time I will make a suggestion is when I see a potential difficulty with getting everyone gathered close, such as in a tight bathroom or on a staircase landing or when a pet may remain in an awkward position. If the pet is difficult to move, then wherever they are is fine. The following is a list of the pros and cons of performing euthanasia indoors versus outdoors.

Inside

Pros – Weather is not a factor

Fewer outdoor distractions – insects, traffic, etc.

Comfortable places – bed, couch, carpeting

Easy to set the stage – music, candles, incense, photos

Other indoor pets present

Clients have other rooms to escape to if needed

Cons – Household interruptions
(e.g., phone calls, TVs, fax machines, doorbells)

Bodily release upon death is a concern (must be contained)

Outside

Pros – Bodily release at death less of a concern

Location options – yard, local park, near burial site

Cons – Uncontrollable factors
(e.g., neighbors, garbage trucks, barking dogs)

Weather can change quickly

Visibility may be difficult

Sedation can take longer due to distractions

Choosing where to gather is very difficult for some people. The place will harbor lasting memories and be the final place their living pet occupies on earth. The family may look upon the place of death with great sadness, and that may affect their decision as to where it should be done. In warm weather, it is nice to be outside under the trees or on the front porch. On colder days, being in front of the fireplace is very comforting. When my opinion is sought, I usually recommend a place where the pet is comfortable, such as its bed or the place it spends the most time. No matter where the euthanasia is done, we need to be mindful that this is now a place of remembrance.

When inside, the family can turn off phones, televisions, computers, etc. to eliminate distractions. If they are expecting more people to arrive, it is best to wait until everyone is present before proceeding. In my experience, the doorbell is the worst interruption because it gets any other pets riled up and is difficult to ignore. It then takes some time to get everyone settled again and ready to proceed. Families may also want to set the stage for a peaceful passing. Soft music, candles, and incense are popular, as are poems and prayers to read. Children often like to surround their pet with special toys, blankets, and treats. In general, anything is acceptable as long as you are able to do your job properly and the pet is comfortable.

When gathering outside, the biggest factor will be the weather. Precipitation is an obvious problem, although I have euthanized in the rain and snow when necessary. Windy days can also be challenging, and I usually recommend that we gather inside instead of being blown around. Pets have a harder time sedating when the elements are not cooperating. The temperature may be too hot or too cold for the comfort of a sick or elderly pet. When it comes down to it, the pet is your patient and you need to decide what is in its best interest.

Another outdoor factor to consider is the time of day. It may be too dark outside by the time you arrive. If the family still wants to be outside, ask for a flashlight to guide you as you prepare to euthanize. I usually keep it off except for when I place the catheter. Euthanizing at night can be very peaceful, and too much light ruins the setting. During the day, there might be barking dogs next door, people working nearby, etc. Take a moment to survey your area and choose the best location.

When

When should euthanasia take place? This will depend on a combination of many factors already discussed, such as who can be there at a particular time, what time of the day is best to be outdoors, etc. Some families like to schedule a euthanasia appointment days in advance and some will request same day service. It can be very hard to wait for "the day" to arrive. It is sometimes helpful to schedule just before a weekend or holiday so that the family has some time to grieve before heading back to work or school.

From the veterinarian's standpoint, the 'when' factor should reflect mostly on the patient. I always want to help a pet before they are in a critical state. Help the family understand the course of the disease, before crisis sets in, through phone consultations, literature handouts, etc. If the family is not ready to euthanize and you feel the pet is suffering, you can offer hospice care to make the pet as comfortable as possible until they are ready to proceed. This may include fluid therapy, pain management, nutrition recommendations, physical therapy, and more. These options are particularly important if the family does not have a veterinarian with whom they already work. Our service gives information to families about particular diseases so that they understand what to expect from their pet as the end of life approaches. This way, the family can make informed decisions and help eliminate needless suffering.

In conclusion, families need to think about what is most important to them as they say goodbye. If they over prepare, and things don't go according to the plan, they are setting themselves up for disappointment. Emotions run incredibly high at these times, and the littlest thing that goes wrong may send them over the edge. Try to keep everything reasonable, relatively simple, and in perspective. No matter what happens, go with the flow and everything should turn out fine in the end.

Making Preparations – Doctor

As I mentioned earlier, preparation is very important to ensure things run smoothly for you. Keeping your vehicle clean, your supplies ready, and knowing your routes will help you utilize your day efficiently. As the saying goes "Failing to plan is planning to fail."

One of the most important things you can do to get an appointment off on the right foot is to be punctual. Have a good system in place to ensure that you are on time for every appointment. If you are just starting out with a mobile service, take time to learn your community and its roads. Know which zip code and area code goes with each area that you will be serving and understand how long it will take you to travel there.

Keep your day on schedule by giving yourself enough time to travel to appointments, maybe get some lunch in between calls, and drop off some referral gifts or a deceased pet to the crematory. As you perform more in-home euthanasias, you will find yourself falling into a comfortable pattern and will know how long a typical appointment will take. You can then plan your next appointment based on that. For example, most of my appointments last 45 to 60 minutes. When I schedule my day, I generally allow for 1.5 hours per appointment so that I have time to travel to the next home. I will allow 2 hours if the appointment is further away. You will have to study your area and know how long you like to take with each family to best establish your schedule.

Have as much prepared prior to your appointment as possible. Your vehicle should be ready to go, your bag fully stocked, clippers charged, paperwork filled out, etc. I also like to draw up my sedation and euthanasia solution before entering the house whenever possible. I keep my stethoscope in my vehicle at all times so that it doesn't get left behind. It is not the end of the world if you forget it, since there are other signs of death besides a quiet heart, but it is comforting to have it with you at all times.

Consider keeping the following items in the vehicle:

Clean towels and blankets

Stretcher

Cleaning wipes or disinfectant spray

Body bags and boxes

Extra sedative and euthanasia solution locked away

Crematory paperwork and entry keys

Local area map or GPS

Notepad and pen

Binder with information on local veterinary clinics

Kleenex®

Cell phone charger and hands-free devices

Extra brochures, business cards, and keepsake items (e.g., clay for paw prints)

Hospice care supplies

Setting the Stage

Being invited into a family's home to help them through this difficult time is a real honor. For most people, in-home euthanasia will be a new experience. They may have witnessed an in-clinic euthanasia before and have decided that this time, they want things to be easier for their beloved pet. They hope the process will run smoothly, but really aren't sure what to expect. Most people have never had a veterinarian in their home, and if they have, maybe it was for something a little less emotional. Either way, it is important for you to convey compassion, confidence, and control: compassion for their situation and for their pet, confidence that you know what you are doing, and control of any situation that might arise throughout the entire appointment.

When you arrive at the home, park nearby to protect the family's privacy. If you know the pet will be leaving with you, you can back into the driveway, unless it is full of cars, which will force you to park with the back of your vehicle next to a walkway or front door. This makes the transition of the pet to your vehicle easier. If the family needs you to take the pet immediately following death, having your vehicle properly positioned will save time.

As you approach the home, have all of your supplies with you and walk slowly with reverence. DO NOT RING THE DOORBELL, but rather knock softly but firmly to announce your arrival. When the family comes to the door, try to mirror their behavior. If they are warm and smiling, be the same. If they are crying and clearly hanging by a thread, offer a supportive hug and empathy. This is your first impression for new clients, and you need them to trust you and feel confident they are in good hands. Set the stage for safe mourning. If you have the desire, you can hang a DO NOT DISTURB sign on the front door to fend off solicitors during your time with the family.

I like to look upon my presence in the home as a friend who has come to help, not as a guest whom they need to "host." Try to be at ease during your stay, blend in, and be comfortable. If you are relaxed, hopefully the family will be too.

In-Home Pet Euthanasia Techniques

Euthanizing a dear pet is about as stressful as it gets for animal lovers, and clients need you to be their rock. I was called out to help a Springer Spaniel named Lacey that had developed metastatic cancer. The young couple who owned her knew that when Lacey started having a hard time breathing, they had to do something. I arrived and sat down on the floor to let their three dogs smell me. The man and woman sat down too and we talked about how wonderful Lacey was and about how devastating this decision was for everyone. We were talking like old friends.

The woman then shared a sad story that had shaped her view of euthanasia. When she first got Lacey, she took her to the vet's office for her puppy vaccines. As she waited, she could hear the family in the next room preparing to euthanize their basset hound. The basset apparently howled loudly through the whole procedure, and she could hear the family crying. The experience was so traumatic for her, that for the next 11 years of Lacey's life, the woman had lived in absolute fear of the day that she might be in a similar position. She was terrified that Lacey would vocalize in pain and be afraid.

Hearing this, I did my best to assure her that Lacey would be at ease and comfortable. The woman's stress was apparent in her every movement, but I stayed quiet and calm in an effort to ease some of her tension. Some pets get very nervous around nervous owners, but Lacey seemed oblivious to her owner's distress. I gave Lacey her sedative and just as she was beginning to relax, the doorbell rang, which sent the dogs into a frenzy. Lacey barked and wanted to get up to see who was at the door. Seeing this, the woman completely broke down. She started screaming at the person to get out and said that everything was turning into a nightmare. She was sweating, shaking, and absolutely devastated. I just spoke softly and stroked Lacey's back and told her what a good dog she was. I told her how nice it was that she had the energy to give some good barks with her fellow dogs. Now of course, Lacey was doing great and when the commotion was over, she simply laid back down and fell asleep. The woman finally took a few deep breaths, was calmed a bit by her husband, and then was able to continue.

Lacey died very peacefully on her bed and never made a sound. When I was getting ready to leave, the woman thanked me for being such a calming presence. She said Lacey's passing was perfect and better than she had imagined. It was like she had already forgotten about the doorbell incident. The moment she had feared for 11 years was over, and she was already making peace with it. It was wonderful to see.

A final note – The man at the door was delivering sympathy flowers for the family. We placed them next to Lacey as she died.

There are some things to take care of before beginning the euthanasia to help ensure that the appointment runs as smoothly as possible. Once the paperwork is complete, it is time to prepare the family. Recommend they turn off their phones if they want extra privacy. The easiest way to do this for home phones is to unplug the phone base from the phone jack in the wall. Taking it "off the hook" leads to beeping that can continue for some time.

If you need to move the pet, determine where the family would like to gather and help them prepare the area. However, try to keep the pet wherever it wants to be. If the room is crowded with furniture, you may need to move a coffee table, plant stand, etc. If your vehicle is not large enough to hold a stretcher, I recommend offering a blanket for large dogs to lie on. You can lift the dog on the blanket for the transition out to the vehicle once euthanasia is complete. Decide which, if any, other pets will be there and get them settled close by, but leave ample room for the rest of the family to gather.

When everyone is present and the pet is comfortable, then you can settle in too. Find a place that gives you easy access to the pet without being too obtrusive. For dogs, I like to sit near the hind end since I usually place catheters in the back leg. I can set my bag off to the side and hidden from view as much as possible. When it comes time to place the catheter, I will lay out my supplies close to the bag and away from the pet's legs (sometimes they give a little myoclonal kick during sedation). Keep everything contained to a small area so it is easy to pack up when you're done.

Bring a towel or small blanket into every appointment. You will need something to place underneath the pet once it is lying down. There is always the concern that the bladder or bowels may release upon death. You can tuck the towel beneath the hind end of dogs or lay it completely under cats. I keep my towel next to my bag until I am  ready to place it under the sedated pet. The towel or blanket you use should be thick enough to absorb a lot of urine and be free of stains, holes, or other blemishes.

If the family has made some preparations, you might see candles, incense, flowers, and other items arranged within the room. Help the family make the setting meaningful by assisting them with proper placement of these things. It is a nice touch the families will remember.

Sedation/Anesthesia

When we think about assisting an animal with euthanasia, the terms "peaceful" and "pain free" hopefully come to mind. After all, the term euthanasia means "good death." There are many factors to consider when preparing to help an animal achieve a good death. How can I make it as pain free as possible? How can I reduce stress? Will it be quick? The whole premise behind in-home euthanasia is to help the animal die in as comfortable a manner as possible, and sedation is a great way to facilitate that. My patients all receive sedation unless their medical condition dictates otherwise.

Sedation is wonderful on so many levels. First and foremost, it makes everything more pleasant for the pet. Families choose euthanasia because their pets are hurting and sedation takes that hurt away. It is their time to be as relaxed as they can be. I often hear people say "It is so nice to see her sleeping. She hasn't been this comfortable in weeks."

Second, sedation helps the family gathered with their pet. It gives them a time for physical contact. When an animal is hurting, it often resents being petted, and the family misses the connection that only touch can bring. Or, a family may have a pet that never liked to be held and now, when the pet is sleeping, they can do that for the first time. What a beautiful experience for them.

Lastly, sedation makes the veterinarian's work easier. There is no need to restrain the pet for catheter placement or worry about pain from the final injection. In fact, the American Veterinary Medical Association's euthanasia guidelines suggest that any method of euthanasia, for any species, is acceptable if the animal in question is sedated first. For me, that speaks volumes on its benefits. Also, my own service is "doctor only." We do not bring technicians so a quiet sleeping pet is important.

There is a distinct difference between sedation and anesthesia; however the terms are commonly interchanged. Sedation means that the pet's ability to react normally to its environment is altered, but it generally does not go to the point of unconsciousness with absolutely no ability to respond to stimuli such as pain, noise, or light. What this means is sedation by itself may allow the pet to awaken when stimulated enough. Anesthesia, however, indicates that the pet has entered a stage of complete unconsciousness and cannot awaken until the drugs begin to be cleared from the body.

There are five stages of anesthesia:

I. Voluntary Excitement – The pet is hypersensitive to noise and touch while losing consciousness. Gentle touch and a quiet presence are important.

II. Involuntary Excitement – This is considered an unpredictable time. If held too long in this stage, the pet may be disorientated, vocalize, bite, leg paddle, and move sporadically.

III. Anesthesia – This is considered a surgical level of anesthesia with the pet unconscious, and in its deepest phase, has no response to internal or external stimuli. Vital functions remain intact and are considered easily reversible.

IV. Medullary Paralysis – This happens when the surgical plane of anesthesia becomes too deep and the pet is overdosing. It is life threatening.

V. Cardiac Arrest – The heart stops beating.
(Some literature combine stages four and five together)

The goal of pre-euthanasia sedation and anesthesia is to reach stage three safely and easily. For euthanasia itself, the pet should move smoothly through all five stages. Barbiturates like pentobarbital are effectively overdosing the pet to reach stage five. For our purposes, we choose sedative and anesthesia drugs to allow the pet to be pain free and comfortable before euthanasia.

Before offering in-home euthanasia to your patients, I highly recommend becoming very familiar with the AVMA's euthanasia guidelines. They were compiled by experts in their respective fields and are designed to alleviate animal suffering around the time of death. If you practice the euthanasia methods in the guide as they are written, you will be protected should something go wrong. New guidelines will be published in 2011 and will specify which techniques are allowed with and without sedation.

The content in this section refers only to the euthanasia of dogs, cats, and some exotics. As veterinarians, it is our job to assess each patient individually and make the decision for or against sedation based on its needs and physical limitations. Each practice should tailor its standards of care around the comfort level and expertise of the staff.

Dogs

An individual dog's reaction to a standard sedation protocol can vary from what is expected. Breed differences, health, size, and weight all seem to affect how things will go. The important thing is to find a protocol that you are comfortable with and use it except when a patient's condition requires a change. Choose a sedative that is easy to administer and induces sleep quickly with minimal side effects.

In my experience, smaller dogs tend to sedate more quickly than do larger individuals, and working breeds tend to resist falling asleep more than other breeds. Border collies, Australian shepherds, and heelers are examples. These breeds like to know what is going on around them and often work to stay awake as long as they can. And for some reason, chows seem to take longer than any other breed, especially if you are outside.

If a dog is taking a long time to relax, I try not to give the impression that he or she is "fighting" the sedation. I will say things like "He just wants to soak up all this love" or "She is a bit dehydrated and we'll just massage the area to help work things in."

Physically speaking, a healthier dog often takes longer to sedate than a sicker one. Sicker, more painful dogs seem to welcome the calming effects quicker. Choose a location on the dog where you can give the sedative injection quickly and effectively, while providing room for the family to offer their pet love. Have the family help you hold the dog if needed, but only if they can do so safely. Many of your patients will be too sick to stand, but some may still be very mobile and active. I like to have owners hold small dogs on their laps with the majority of the dog's body held close to the owner's abdomen or chest. Small dogs are used to being held in this way. Bigger dogs can be held in the same manner as you would when giving a vaccine; someone up front to hold the head with you at the rear.

If your patient is aggressive, you may use a muzzle, but most clients don't like this. They have chosen in-home euthanasia to keep their dogs comfortable, and a muzzle sends the wrong message. Use your instincts to tell you which pet has the potential to bite. These dogs often watch you very closely and turn to face you every chance they get, either because they are scared or agitated by all the emotion in the room. Some dogs are very protective of their owners and will bite if you get too close. Keeping dog psychology in mind, we must remember we are in their territory now. If you suspect that a dog might bite, talk to the owner. See the chapter on "Potential Problems" for more tips on handling aggressive pets.

Routes

Choosing an injection site depends on how the dog is positioned and whether or not you are injecting intramuscularly (IM) or subcutaneously (SQ). Good IM injection sites include the thigh muscles, epaxial muscles in the lumbar region, or the triceps. I prefer to use the epaxial muscles because dogs seem less aware of injections in this area. Administer the injection slowly and with a constant, even pressure. To help lessen the surprise of the injection, scratch and rub the area before inserting the needle. The needle should go in quickly. Use the smallest needle you can and aim directly down into the middle of the muscle. Remember your anatomical landmarks to avoid large nerves, blood vessels, or bone. If your dog is already in pain, he shouldn't notice an IM injection too much. Small dogs tend to be more sensitive to IM injections, so for them, I prefer the SQ route.

Good SQ sites are found anywhere on the body that is covered with loose skin and where you can avoid fat. Again, rub the area to desensitize the dog to your touch, and when ready, tent the skin to create your SQ pocket. Make sure you are injecting under and not into the skin. Intradermal injections hurt and the dog will let you know that you are not where you should be. If necessary, redirect your needle deeper or switch out your needle and try in another place. Make sure you always use new, sharp needles to keep injection pain to a minimum. A SQ injection feels the same as receiving a vaccination so that is how I describe it to families.

Any injection site will benefit from being massaged to help increase blood flow and relieve pain. Increasing blood flow can be important if you think systemic perfusion is already low. I have found no evidence that giving an injection far from the heart will slow sedative uptake so give it where you feel is best and massage. I rub the area before injecting to lessen the surprise and to improve blood flow to the area and continue massaging afterwards to speed absorption. If the family can do this, even better.

For the first two years of my service, I gave IM injections to all of my patients thinking that they would sedate more quickly this way. That is, until I met a small blind dog that I just knew was going to hate it. I decided to go SQ, and he relaxed down just as quickly as he would have with an IM injection. From that point on, SQ has been my preferred method. Whatever route you pick, avoid injecting into fat deposits, which will slow down the absorption rate of your drug and keep in mind that some sedatives might sting more than others.

Some practitioners like to give oral sedatives to relax their canine patients. You can give acepromazine, diazepam, or some other sedative to fractious dogs, but most of the time they are unnecessary. In the rare instance I give them, I double the typical dose and have the family feed them to the dog two hours before I arrive. I will then give more sedative via injection.

Protocols

There are many different sedation protocols you can use for your canine patients. The one you choose should depend on your preferred depth of sedation and the overall condition of the dog in question. Heart rate, blood pressure, hydration status, pain, exhaustion, and organ function all play a role. These factors also help determine how much sedative to give. Your veterinary education taught you all of the types of drugs, their interactions with each other, and side effects, but it is your personal experience that dictates what the best choice is for you. After three years offering in-home euthanasia, I still use the same protocol for dogs I started with because I understand what I can expect for every type of dog and their condition.

It is helpful to have a variety of drugs in your drug box so you can be ready for whatever the day brings. When choosing which drugs you will carry, try to keep in mind their use with other species like cats, rodents, rabbits, birds, large animals, etc. It is nice to carry only a few drugs but still be prepared for multiple situations. Below is a list of drugs to consider. Besides their excellent sedation and analgesia properties, I use most of them because they keep nicely in my drug box for a long period of time. I also carry large animal concentrations of drugs so the volume I administer is reduced.

Some of my protocol drugs are listed along with fellow practitioner's preferred drugs:

- Alpha2-agonists
  (e.g., xylazine or dexmedetomidine)
- Alpha2-agonist reversals
  (e.g., Yohimbine® or atipamazole)
- Phenothiazines
  (e.g., acepromazine)
- Opioids
  (e.g., butorphanol, nalbuphine, or Fentanyl®)
- Dissociatives
  (e.g., tiletamine/zolazepam (Telazol®) or ketamine)
- Benzodiazepines
  (e.g., diazepam or midazolam)

Dogs can be sedated with a variety of drugs. They handle alpha2-agonists, dissociatives, opioids, and phenothiazines well. I like to use a combination of xylazine and butorphanol or nalbuphine mixed with acepromazine for the vast majority of my canine patients. This allows for good, deep sedation that can be partially reversed with yohimbine if the family changes their mind at the last minute. All three of these drugs can be combined in a single syringe, given IM or SQ, and typically take effect within about five minutes.

An alpha2-agonist and opioid work well in combination, but dogs are sometimes arouseable. The added acepromazine helps to keep the dog in a state of deep sleep. If the Alpha2-agonist/opioid combination is not strong enough, it is better to add a third drug rather than simply giving higher doses of the Alpha2-agonist or opioid because you risk inducing vomiting and dramatically lowering the dog's blood pressure. This combination produces a nice consistent level of sedation that I can rely on. The drugs do not lower blood pressure to the point where I have difficulties with catheter placement. I also like the added acepromazine because its yellow

color helps distinguish my sedative syringes from my saline flush syringes. One of my associates uses a similar protocol but likes to add Atropine to the syringe to keep the heart rate up. She feels that the dogs' blood pressures are higher, which makes catheter placement easier for her.

Another doctor in my service likes to use SQ Telazol® combined with acepromazine and a micro dose of xylazine to sedate dogs. I have also used this protocol and find that the dogs sedate very nicely. If a dissociative drug is used by itself, it can produce an excitatory phase. Adding the acepromazine and Alpha-2 leads to a much smoother sedation. This protocol is also good to use when cardiac output is questionable. It tends to keep the heart rate normal to elevated and blood pressure up. This being said, I can place a catheter on just about any dog in any condition. When I train new doctors, however, they do seem to find veins better with this Telazol® combination protocol.

I also give a little Telazol® on top of my Alpha2/opioid/acepromazine combo if I have to switch from a planned IV euthanasia to an intracardiac or intrahepatic route. I want my patients to be truly anesthetized for these procedures so they will not feel my injection at all. Telazol®, or ketamine if you prefer, is a good additional sedative to give a dog that is overriding an Alpha2-agonist.

There are a few potential side effects when using an Alpha2. If a dog has a very strong urge to urinate or defecate, you may see it raise its head every once and awhile. Dogs can also be very sensitive to sound when under the influence of an Alpha 2, which can increase the time needed for sedation to take effect, especially if you are gathered in a noisy place. An example of this would be a dog that is resting comfortably, snoring even, and then sits up when you turn on your clippers to prepare the catheter site. In this instance, I would turn them off, wait a few more moments, and then try again. Most dogs will not react the second time. If they do, you have two options. You can forgo the clipper use or give more sedative. If you have already given a full dose of the Alpha-2, then try something else like a dissociative IM. As the dog relaxes, it is common to see some involuntary leg movements and minor muscle twitches. Vomiting is a big concern with Alpha2s; however I still find the incidence quite rare. Even the sickest dog will not always vomit.

Some vets like to use a 2-step sedation protocol. They will give a sedative like nalbuphine and acepromazine followed a few minutes later with something like SQ or IM Telazol® or even IV propofol or thiopental to induce anesthesia. True anesthesia drugs like these, when given just before euthanasia, should eliminate almost all agonal breathing and most reflexive movements. Whatever your preference, study the drugs' effects and know what you are working with. Ask around to learn what has been working well for other vets. Two-step protocols lead to wonderful anesthesia, but they do take longer. You will have to decide what is important to your clients. In my experience, as long as their dog is peaceful, and things progress in a timely fashion, the details are not important to them.

The Onset of Sedation

There is a natural progression to sedation, and once the drugs start to take effect, you should see a nice gentle transition. Once you have given the injection, talk the family through what they can expect. My standard speech goes something like "Now as he starts to relax, he will essentially just lay his head down and fall asleep. He may take some deep breaths or give some deep sighs and you may even see him move his legs a little like he's dreaming. His eyes will probably always be a little open and they will through euthanasia as well. This is very natural".

This sedation time is very powerful for the family. It will be their last time to communicate love to their canine friend and many families want to get in lots of hugs and kisses. Let them give all the love the dog can easily handle. As wonderful as tender touches for the dog can be, sometimes less is more. In an effort to let the dog focus on himself rather than the goings on around him, you might have to limit excessive family contact until he is clearly sedated. If you see your patient is having a hard time relaxing, make a suggestion for the family to pet the dog very slowly and restrict petting to the top of the head or neck. Avoid the face, ventral chest, and feet.

If the dog is standing while sedating, sit nearby and be ready to offer support as he lies down. You might need to help guide him by gently applying pressure on his haunches to direct his seat or move his front legs forward to slide him down. I avoid touching the belly or ventral chest so he senses a clear path to the floor/bed. Take your time with this. Some dogs just need extra time to relax and you don't want to appear like you are rushing things along if your patient is not ready.

Before proceeding with catheter placement or direct venipuncture, assess the depth of sedation. Dogs will often take a few deep sighs and have some minor leg movements. When deep enough in sleep, there should be little to no palpebral reflex, no tail tucking when the caudal thigh is touched, and no withdrawal reflex when the toe is pinched. I tend to tickle in between the toes to check the depth of sedation.

To prepare the family if vomiting is a possibility, you can say: "I know that he has been nauseous. The sedative will not take the urge away if it comes. If he acts sick, we will just support him through it and then he will feel much better." Again, vomiting is very rare, but it does happen. If the dog wants to get up in mid-sedation due to nausea, keep him in his spot and place a towel under his mouth to catch whatever comes. Most of the time, it will be only a small amount of bile.

If the dog feels the urge to urinate or defecate, this will slow the onset of sedation. He may appear to be well on his way into deep sleep when suddenly he sits up and acts like he wants to leave the area. Don't let him. Keep him close by so family members don't have to scramble around and get resituated. I like to gently remind the family that there is a towel under the hind end or at least one close by if needed. If the dog does get up, go with him and offer support. You may need to hold him up while he relieves himself and then guide him back to the chosen location. Some dogs will be too groggy to make it back and you will have to move your supplies to their new resting place. Most often what happens is the dog feels the urge to potty and then once he is up and moving around, he just wants to lie back down. Limit the disturbance by keeping him in one spot. If a dog releases his bowels and it needs to be cleaned up, collect it in your towel, then tuck the towel over to hide the feces for the rest of the appointment.

If at any point the dog appears to be in distress while sedated, move forward with euthanasia rapidly. When dealing with dyspneic dogs, I always gather my euthanasia supplies together quickly so that if the dyspnea worsens, I am ready. In some cases, sedation alone may be enough to bring about euthanasia, and if you suspect that this may be occurring, let the family know. Offer comforting words and give them confidence that you are not going to let their pet suffer. If you are calm, families will be as well.

If the dog has been having seizures, let the family know that he may have one at anytime during the process. For these dogs, once I give the sedative, I get my supplies together and am prepared to euthanize immediately if a seizure appears imminent. Only one time in my career has a dog seizured during sedation that had never had one before. About two minutes into sedation, the dog went into a grand mal seizure. I cannot say the sedative caused it, but I'm sure it didn't help. I happened to have a vet student with me so she held him tight while I euthanized. Fortunately the owner had stepped out of the room and missed most of the drama. Only a very small percentage of seizure-prone dogs will have one during sedation and euthanasia. As with any ill patient, alter your protocol accordingly, including forgoing sedation altogether if necessary.

Cats

In general, cats do not like to be handled by a stranger and my rule of thumb is to limit my contact with them if they appear agitated at all. I give them their space for as long as I can before proceeding with sedation. Give the injection quickly but gently, then sit back and let the owner comfort them as they need. Some cats will not even notice an injection. Others will howl and cry at the slightest touch, which can make for a stressful encounter. Families are hoping that the entire euthanasia experience will be easy on their cat, and this includes the sedation injection. I have not figured out how to perfectly predict which cat will get upset and which will not, so I always move gently, slowly, and quietly.

Prepare the family for what might occur before proceeding with sedation. They need to know that their cat may not like the injection, especially if it is given in the muscle. I tell families that the cat will likely notice the injection, but how they react to it is up to them, and if the cat growls or hisses, it is directed at me, not the family. If the cat has a very sweet demeanor and has always handled injections well at the vet's office, the family will expect that in the home as well. However, they need to understand that if your injection goes in the muscle or if the sedative stings, the cat is more likely to notice it.

When giving a cat an injection, always keep safety in the front of your mind. Cat bites and scratches commonly lead to infections and that is the last thing you want the family to remember. Make sure the person holding the cat is comfortable doing so, is in a good position, and using both hands. They can stroke the cat during the injection, but if the cat lurches forward, they should be ready to tighten their hold.

Finding a place to give an injection in a cat that is being cradled by its owner can be difficult. For our purposes, the best place is where you can move quickly and keep the cat stable and secure. Most of my clients like to hold their cats near their chest, close to their heart. I usually give the injection in the thigh or neck region and use my other hand to gently massage the neck. This way, if the cat lunges forward, I can quickly grab the scruff and help keep them in place. The client then holds on a little tighter and we can love on the cat until we feel him starting to relax.

If you know the cat you're helping is going to be upset, prepare the room ahead of time. Close closet doors, hallway doors, etc. in an effort to eliminate escape routes. You can then give the sedative and let go so no one gets hurt. You want your feline patient to remain close by so you can watch the sedation progress while still giving the cat the space it wants. Hopefully it will find a quiet place in the room to settle down. While the cat starts to relax, you can draw up more sedative and have it ready in case you need it, particularly if you are unsure if the cat actually got the full, initial dose. As the cat is relaxing, give the family an opportunity to share some nice stories about their pet. After a few minutes, you can check on its progress and when appropriate, bring it back to the designated place for euthanasia.

> *I was called out to help a cat awhile back that, for all intents and purposes, was a feral cat living in a farmhouse. The owner did not want to be present and asked if I would be able to handle things on my own. I calmly assured her that I would be just fine and that her cat would be kept as comfortable as I could make it. When I entered the bedroom, the cat was lying underneath the bed, right in the center as far from my reach as possible. I tried for just a minute or so to see if she would come to me. She, of course, would not. Having been at this type of service for some time, I knew that by myself, I would not be able to isolate her easily. This was a time to be creative. I took off the bedspread and pillows, lifted up the mattress, and rested it up against the wall leaving about 10 inches of space between the bottom of it and the wall itself. I pushed one end up tightly to the perpendicular wall to create a trap for her. I then lifted up the box spring and placed it up against the mattress. The cat, having its best hiding spot taken away,*

In-Home Pet Euthanasia Techniques

quickly dove into the space I created between mattress and wall. With sedative syringe in hand, I got down on all fours and crept up to her under the mattress. She had nowhere to hide and gave me no resistance at all. I was rather proud of myself. As she sedated, I remade the bed and euthanized when she was ready for me. When I rejoined the owner in the other room, it was nice to tell her that things went smoothly. There was no crying or wailing, thrashing or scratching. The owner was so pleased. She had been putting off the appointment for so long because she didn't want a difficult confrontation. Had this cat been ferocious with me, I would have placed a towel over her too.

Tips on feline sedation:

1. If the cat does not want to be held, keep the cat close to the ground when giving the injection to prevent a fall.
2. Dehydrated cats may take longer to fully sedate.
3. Be careful when rubbing an intramuscular injection site. It might be painful.
4. If the cat is moving around while falling asleep and still isn't ready to be held, you can place a towel or light blanket over it for a calming effect.
5. Oral pre-sedation with acepromazine, given by the owner before you arrive does not always work and can make the cat more agitated.
6. SQ administration of Telazol® lessens the "lip-licking" that is often seen when this drug is given IM.

Routes

Like dogs, cats can receive sedation through IM or SQ injections. Almost any protocol you choose will work well either way. Early in my service, I gave all cats IM injections in an effort to speed the onset of sleep. However, I now find that full sedative effects set in just as fast with the SQ route. My veterinary team is currently conducting a study on euthanasia in cats with a sedation protocol of Telazol® and acepromazine. Preliminary results show that cats sedate down an average of one minute longer with SQ injections versus IM. Since SQ injections tend to irritate the cat less, the extra time to full sedation is well worth it for a smoother euthanasia appointment. If you choose to use the IM route, the thigh muscles work well. SQ injections are best given at the base of the neck where the skin is loosest.

Protocols

The level of sedation you need for your feline patients will depend on your method of euthanasia. Some veterinarians use a 2-step sedation protocol, while others use a 1-step method. A 2-step protocol might include an acepromazine/butorphanol combination SQ followed by Telazol® or ketamine/diazepam IM. The 2-step protocol will take longer because you have to wait for the first injection to take full effect before you give the second. Some families do not like the extra waiting. An example of a 1-step protocol would be Telazol® only or Telazol® mixed with acepromazine given SQ or IM. In general, if you explain your methods and reasons for them, the family will be happy.

Once you have a sedation protocol you like, I recommend using it for most of your appointments. You will have more confidence knowing what to expect and can better handle variations from the norm. For the past three years, I have had great success with a 1-step Telazol®/acepromazine combination. I know of practitioners who reconstitute Telazol® with Fentanyl®, other opioids, or dexmedetomidine instead of sterile water.

Telazol® can be painful if given too quickly so I inject slowly whenever possible. Most cats do not notice it, or if they do, they react mildly. Almost all cats will jump if you push it fast. Adding another drug into the syringe containing the Telazol® seems to lessen the sting of the injection and helps smooth the process of sedation. A colleague has reported that adding Fentanyl® might lessen the sting of injection. Regardless of where you give Telazol®, tissue damage from the needle may cause the cat to react when you pull it out.

Two things are interesting to note about Telazol®. For our purposes, it does not need to be refrigerated as indicated on the bottle. It holds up just fine for weeks at room temperature. It also works well when given SQ, despite being labeled for IM use only.

The Onset of Sedation

I like the intrarenal method of feline euthanasia, and therefore my cats need to be completely anesthetized. The Telazol®/acepromazine combination works fast, usually in about three to four minutes, is predictable, and puts the cat in a nice plane of anesthesia. Typical signs that the drugs are starting to take effect include licking the lips, pupil dilation, mild to moderate head weave, quieting of the tail, and a relaxed demeanor. As with dogs, vomiting during the onset of sedation can occur. Fortunately, this has happened to my feline patients only a few times. Once the cat is in a deep sleep, there should be no response to stimuli. I usually pinch the toes and test for deep pain before proceeding with euthanasia. Another way to assess relaxation and deep sedation is to palpate the abdomen. If the cat resists your touch and tightens its abdominal wall muscles, then he is not deep enough to ensure a pain free passing. When this happens, I will wait a little longer or give a little more sedative. They will not feel another sedation injection and it will help speed things along.

If you prefer intravenous euthanasia in cats, you may be content with only light sedation. Make sure the cat is calm enough to allow you to stretch out their leg, place a tourniquet or hold off the vein, clip hair if necessary, and then place the catheter or needle. No one likes to see a struggle, especially a grieving family. On occasion, you may help a cat that already has a catheter in place from the referring veterinarian. If this is the case, there really is no need to give a sedative, but you certainly can if you want. The cat may resist being held and petted by the family without it. You can give acepromazine, an opiate, or even something like Telazol® through the IV. If you do give Telazol®, be prepared that the cat might react for a split second and lurch forward. Gently restrain the cat while you are injecting, just like a technician would in the clinic when you are inducing anesthesia.

While your feline patient is relaxing, a family member can hold him, brush him, or snuggle up close. Cats love to lie in the sun, and I often find myself performing euthanasia near a window or out in the grass. Unlike dogs, cats usually relax down quickly whether they are inside or out. If you are outdoors, make sure the cat is completely sedated before you trust him to stay put. You would hate to find yourself running after a disoriented cat.

Exotics

There are many different kinds of exotic pets. Rabbits, guinea pigs, rats, and lizards are the most common types I see. I have also helped numerous birds, ferrets, and hamsters. I sedate them with a combination of Telazol® and acepromazine using an intramuscular injection placed in the thigh. Most exotics will sedate deeply within about three to four minutes, similar to cats. If the pet is very small, it may only take 60 seconds. Test for pain response by toe pinching and look for absent palpebral reflexes. The amount I give is very small and can be found in the Drug Protocal PDF in your purchased ebook folder along with other dosing protocols. If you work a lot with exotics, you may want to consider obtaining some inhalant gases like Halothane® or Isoflurane®. The liquid form can be applied to cotton balls and placed by the pet for it to inhale. They will essentially overdose on the inhalant gas. I do not work with exotics enough to utilize this technique; therefore I recommend you research this further if interested. Before you work with exotics, get familiar with their behavior and mannerisms so that you can predict and understand their responses to sedation. For example, rabbits require higher doses than do other exotics and they lick their lips a lot, while lizards may change colors when you inject them.

Catheter Placement

Catheter placement is one of those things that most veterinarians either love or hate. There is rarely an in-between. These days, most educational institutions are teaching veterinary students to place catheters for small animal euthanasias. Proper use of catheters is superior to direct venipuncture in that it guarantees that what you are injecting stays within the bloodstream. You will eliminate the risk of multiple injections when an owner is present. If the pet moves its leg, the catheter will stay put. Direct venipuncture opens the door for the needle to poke through the vein wall and euthanasia solution to flow into the SQ space or neighboring muscle. When this happens, you have to start again causing the family unnecessary stress. Families commonly share with me the horror stories of previous pet euthanasias. I hear things like "The doctor gave the shot in the leg and she took 20 minutes to die" or "It was awful to see her struggle and pull away with all those pokes." With or without sedation, catheter placement is the safest way to ensure an intravenous euthanasia goes smoothly.

Before you begin an in-home euthanasia service, you should be comfortable placing catheters, even if you are planning on performing direct venipuncture or intracardiac or intraabdominal injections. Hopefully your education and clinical work has solidified your technique, but if you are feeling under-prepared, practice at a local clinic or even on your own pets. I once gave my dog a sedative so I could practice catheter placement for about 20 minutes; then I trimmed his nails to justify it. I think he forgave me.

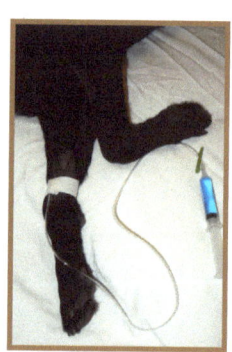

Most in-home euthanasia doctors work alone and therefore need to be able to place a catheter without assistance. Even if you are great at two-person placement, it is different when you are alone. I recommend practicing with a tourniquet and getting used to the different angles involved when you are by yourself, even if you are confident in your technique when you have an assistant. For our purposes, I will talk about placing a catheter in a sedated dog or cat.

In-Home Pet Euthanasia Techniques

Before you begin, take note if your patient is relaxed enough for you to proceed without restraint. Your patient should remain unaware of what you are doing. This means no leg withdrawal when you insert the catheter. Briefly look the pet over to determine whether a front leg or back is your best placement site. The common veins of choice are the cephalic vein, the lateral saphenous vein, or the medial saphenous vein. Most veterinarians have a preferred vein they like to use. The idea is to get the catheter in quickly while still allowing the family to gather closely around their pet. As the pet is falling asleep, ready your supplies. If you think that the sedated pet's blood pressure will drop quickly, get ready to place the catheter as soon as you can.

To help families focus on their pet and not on what I am doing, I like to lay out my supplies on the side of my bag opposite the family. The bag helps to keep everything out of view. The pictures below demonstrate the difference between having your items in view or tucked out of sight. As the family is telling stories or just spending quiet time with their pet, you can pull out the items you need. This can include clippers, tourniquet,

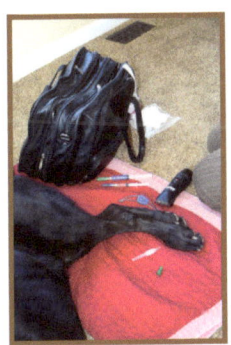 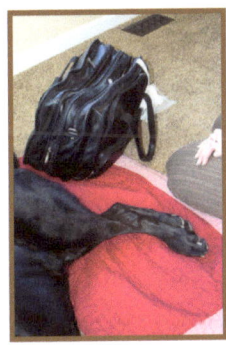

flush, male adaptor or extension set, white tape, trash container, a catheter flushed with sterile saline, euthanasia solution, and cleaning gauze. As you are done with each thing, put it away to keep the area clean. This also reduces the risk of children or pets touching dangerous things. If there are a lot of other pets or kids around, I usually just take items out as I need them and then put them right back in the bag when I am done.

The catheter size you choose will depend on the size of the pet you are helping. For cats and dogs under 30 pounds, I like to use a 24 gauge catheter. The smaller the catheter, the easier it is to place in the vein. Make sure your euthanasia solution is still easy to inject through these small catheters. If necessary, you can mix saline with your solution to thin it out. For larger dogs, I use a 22 gauge catheter because the veins are bigger and I can more rapidly administer the greater volume of euthanasia solution. Always keep a large number of both sizes of catheters in your bag. You never know how many you will need in a given day.

As the pet is sleeping, you can stroke the leg a bit to stimulate circulation. If you are clipping the hair, prepare your catheter site by clipping down to the skin with a #40 or #50 surgical blade. Clip enough hair to allow yourself at least two attempts in the same vein. That way you won't have to clip a second time if the vein blows during your first attempt. The sound of clippers in a quiet room can seem obtrusive. Spend your money on a high quality pair that is quiet and will last a long time. Place your clipped hair in the container you brought for trash and put the clippers back in the bag.

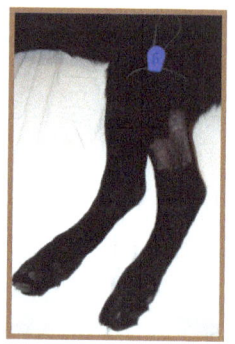

Next, place a tourniquet above your planned catheter site. The tourniquet will have a release of some sort that should be facing you. Find a secure location that will prevent the tourniquet from slipping down and keep the skin taut. For example, I like to use the groove between the tibia and patella when placing a catheter in the back leg of a small dog. Once the tourniquet is tight, squeeze the foot to help the vein to fill. The vein you are using should be easy to see and feel. If the vein is not easy to find, tighten the tourniquet, squeeze the foot, and look again. When necessary, you can switch to another vein all together. Different veins have different characteristics, such as the following.

Lateral Saphenous Vein

Pros – easy to locate

       long length

       away from the head where families like to gather

       perfectly positioned when a pet is lying on its side

Cons – short legs make placement more difficult

       poorer pressures due to distance from heart

       loose skin and minimal fascia to anchor the vein in place

       vein can split into smaller veins

Medial Saphenous Vein

Pros – easy to locate

    medium length

    away from the head

    laterally recumbent body position builds blood volume in the vein

Cons – upper leg has to be moved out of the way

    tourniquet placement more difficult

    works better on cats than dogs

Cephalic Vein

Pros – easy to locate

    usually good diameter

    long length

    good pressures due to proximity to heart

    consistent vein pattern

    lateral recumbency increases blood volume/distension of the lower leg cephalic vein

Cons – harder to place in lateral recumbency

    near the head where families like to gather

When you have picked which vein you will use, position your body for catheter placement. Your stance will depend on the vein you are using. For the saphenous vein, I usually kneel and bend down close. For the cephalic vein, I find myself lying partially on my side in order to be in line with the leg. If the dog or cat is on a higher surface like a couch, you will not have to bend over as far. Whatever your position, just try to be comfortable and relaxed. Instinct will take over and help guide you.

You will probably need to hold the vein in place to minimize lateral movement away from your catheter. For the saphenous vein, which tends to be very "roly-poly," I recommend securing the vein distal to your catheter site with your thumb. Actually place your thumb over the vein and even apply a little tension distally to straighten out any kinks in the vein. You are essentially trapping blood between the tourniquet

In-Home Pet Euthanasia Techniques

and your thumb, hopefully creating a nice target. For the cephalic vein in a laterally recumbent dog, I lay my thumb alongside the vein on the side that is closest to the ground. It looks like I am using the side of my thumb to hold the vein up.

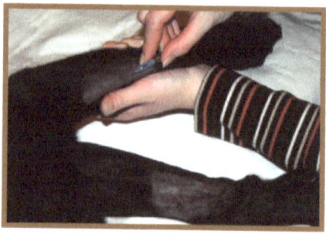
cephalic placement

To be safe, try to place your catheter in the most distal portion of the vein where you can easily see and feel it. If your vein blows, you will have more vein to work with proximally. In fact, it sometimes seems that having the vein blow can actually improve blood pressure in the same vein between the blowout and the tourniquet. If you see that the vein looks better distal to a blowout, you can place your catheter there too if necessary. This goes against everything we learn in school and clinics, but in the case of euthanasia, it is not off limits. The trick is to test your new catheter placement slowly with saline to see how much leakage there is at the blowout site. If there is little to none, which is usually the case, you can administer your euthanasia solution while applying gentle pressure to the area. <u>Only attempt this if the pet is completely sedated</u>. Euthanasia solution can irritate the surrounding tissues if it leaks from the vein. I have never had a pet react adversely to this technique, and I only use it if switching legs will be upsetting to those gathered around.

When you place the catheter, point the bevel up and pierce the skin at a shallow angle. When you see blood in your stylet **and** catheter sheath, you may advance the catheter forward until the hub is against the skin. Then, pull back your stylet to check for blood flow into the hub. Once you are confident you have seated the catheter adequately inside the vein, release your tourniquet, remove the stylet and immediately place it in the trash container. Seal the catheter with either a male adaptor or extension set. If you prefer male adaptors, I recommend ones with luer locks to prevent the adaptor from slipping off the catheter hub. If you prefer extension sets, fill them with saline before placing the catheter and twist them in tightly to prevent leaks. Extension sets made with luer locks are available also.

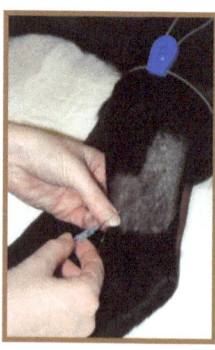
lat. saphenous placement

Now that the catheter is in place, you need to secure it to the leg. Tape works well for this. I use 1inch white tape. I loosely stick a piece to the side of the bag as part of my preparations for catheter placement. That way it's all set when I'm ready to fasten down the catheter. Securely tape in your catheter by including your entire male adapter. If I'm using an extension set, I use two pieces of tape for extra security. Wrap the tape around the leg, covering the point where the catheter enters the skin and then back over where the adaptor or extension set joins the catheter. Squeeze the tape firmly into place. Properly securing the catheter is important so that if the family wants to reposition the pet before proceeding, nothing will slip out of place. If you do not like the look of white tape, you can cover it with Vetwrap®.

Before proceeding with euthanasia, flush the catheter and confirm its proper placement. Let the family know that you are just making sure everything is where you need it and that the pet will not be affected by the injection of sterile saline. You can draw back to see blood if you wish, but this can be a disturbing sight for families, and sometimes the negative pressure will completely collapse the vein and you won't get a flash anyway. I recommend just pushing 1 or 2 mls of saline and looking for the formation of a bleb under the skin. If you feel certain that you are in the vein, but your saline will not flush, pull the catheter back just a tiny bit in case the end is up against a valve or the wall of the vein. If you still cannot get the saline to flow, remove your adaptor or extension and try to reposition your catheter slightly. If you have no success, start over completely, either higher up or on another leg.

More than likely, the family will be watching a good portion of your catheter placement. They know that with every step you complete, they are getting closer to the end. Because of this, it is important not to let them focus too much on the technical aspects of what you are doing. If they are interested in talking, ask them to tell a story about their pet. You can ask them questions. How did Stella come to be with you? Did she come from a big litter? What was her favorite food? How did she get her name? If they prefer quiet time for reflection, just go about your work with soft hands and gentle movements. For the family's sake, I do not go into technical details and describe what I am doing. If the vein blows, I just hold off for a moment, and then try again without bringing attention to it. Your goal is to keep the family as relaxed as possible and confident that you can get the job done. If you have to switch legs, let them know why you are changing positions, and continue as before. Most people are very understanding if things are a bit tricky because of a pet's illness. No worries. If you are relaxed, they will feel it.

So what happens if you cannot get the catheter placed in either the back or front leg on the "up" side of a laterally recumbent dog? Do you need to flip the pet over? Not yet. While you have been working, blood has likely pooled a bit in the cephalic vein in the leg closest to the ground. Clip a small portion of hair over the most distal portion of the cephalic vein, running along the medial surface of the carpus, and a bit proximally as well. You should see a nice vein there. If so, place 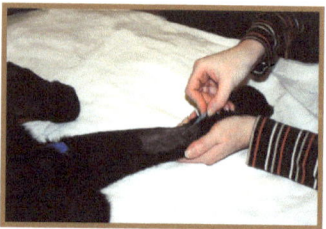 your tourniquet over the antebrachium near the elbow and squeeze the paw. This segment of the cephalic vein is not very "roly-poly" and is easy to use. You can of course work higher up on the leg if you prefer. If the lower leg cephalic vein will not work either, you can then roll the pet over and start again on the other side or perform a cardiac or abdominal injection. I personally have never placed a catheter for euthanasia in the jugular vein of a dog or cat. I don't see why you can't though. It just isn't ideal with the family close to the head and no one to hold the vein off for you. One of my doctors used to place catheters in cats using the medial saphenous vein. The trick is to place the tourniquet high up the thigh to leave you ample room on the vein to work with. She found it easy and effective.

In an in-home euthanasia practice, you will be faced with helping pets that are actively seizuring. To place a catheter under these conditions, use the leg that has the biggest vein or that you feel most comfortable with. I prefer the saphenous vein so that I can be away from the head. If someone is willing to help, have him or her steady the leg for you. With a back leg, have them push the stifle straight, and for the front leg, they can brace the elbow. Front legs tend to extend during seizures, which can be helpful if you are alone. If the legs are paddling too much, give the euthanasia injection into the heart or abdomen. Intracardiac injections are preferred because of their rapid action. Intraabdominal absorption can take a long time, and the pet will continue to seizure in the meantime.

> Not too long ago, I was called to help a dog that was experiencing petite mal seizures. When I got to the home, the young owner was on the floor with the dog trying to keep her calm. The dog was very agitated, trying to bite anyone that

came close and thrashing about. The owner's mother and sister were there asking to help if they could. This dog was just too agitated to sedate, and I didn't want to wait any longer. As I always do, I went ahead to place a catheter in the lateral saphenous vein. With all the extra help around, I knew I could do it. I asked the owner's mother to support the dog's stifle to prevent the leg from pulling away. Quickly, I clipped an area of hair over the vein, inserted the catheter, and injected without flushing or taping it in place. She died immediately, with great relief to us all. Even if I was exceptionally skilled at direct venipuncture, it would have been risky in this dog. If catheter placement was not an option, I would have proceeded with an intracardiac stick and been forced to wait for sedation to take effect since she was never fully unconscious with her seizures.

When it comes to euthanasia, every veterinarian's biggest fear is that the catheter will not work properly when the family is expecting you to proceed. Once the family has prepared themselves that the next injection will be the one that takes their pet's life, we pray that everything will flow smoothly. But what if it doesn't? There are three scenarios that come to mind that will cause you great concern during an appointment.

The first scenario is when you know the catheter is placed within the vein, but the solution will not push in. Causes for this are a kinked catheter, a plug within the tip (either tissue or blood clot), or the tip pressed up against a venous valve or wall. When this happens, pull out the catheter ever so slightly and see if flow resumes. If not, flush a bit with your saline to see if anything gets through. If nothing gets through, place a new catheter proximally and try again. The second scenario is when you begin to push the euthanasia solution into a properly placed catheter and it leaks out around your site. This means that your syringe is not securely attached to your catheter hub or extension. Quickly either squeeze your forefingers around the hub and continue or peel back your tape to anchor the adapter/extension some more. If you already planned on giving more euthanasia solution than the pet actually needed, a little bit leaking out will not affect the time to death. When euthanasia is complete, you can gently wipe away the spilled solution from the skin. The third scenario, and the most troubling to me, is when you believe your catheter is placed correctly, but find a bleb forming as you administer your solution. This can happen even if your saline flush test appears normal. In four years, this has happened to me twice. What makes this scenario challenging is that the bleb makes placing a new catheter proximally very difficult. The SQ bleb obscures your view of the vein and may force you to use another leg. When this happened to me, I just told the family that I was going to give the rest in another leg. I never told them what had happened and they never asked. You have to work quickly so that the misplaced injected solution does not absorb and lower blood pressures. Both times this happened, the sedated pet showed absolutely no response or discomfort and the second catheter placement took no more than 60 seconds.

Butterfly Catheters or Needles

I like using catheters because 99.99% of the time, when I administer euthanasia solution, it flows smoothly into the vein. However, you may prefer to use a needle or butterfly catheter in your appointments. If this is the case, I cannot recommend presedation enough. Placing a straight needle into the vein of an awake pet is very risky as the needle can easily puncture directly through it. The solution will be injected into the SQ space causing your patient great pain and the family unneeded stress and frustration. When people describe a bad euthanasia, this is usually the cause. If the pet is sedated, it should be safe to do. Just beware of myoclonal kicks and unexpected seizures.

One of the benefits of standard catheter placement is the time you can give the family once it is placed. I like to offer the family some private time before I proceed with euthanasia, and if they accept, I can step out of the room with my catheter secured in place. The pet can continue deeper into sedation without me worrying about lower blood pressures. If you use butterfly catheters, you can also do this, but your syringe will have to be attached or an adapter placed to prevent blood backflow. Make sure the length of it is securely taped to the leg.

Euthanasia Techniques

This section will focus on the various euthanasia techniques that an in-home service might use. Over the past 100 years, a lot has been written about euthanasia, but very little concerning actual techniques is available. What veterinarians have written is scattered throughout journals and other literature. The following is a compilation of classic euthanasia techniques for small animals with concise descriptions on how to perform them.

The AVMA euthanasia guidelines provide a long list of acceptable methods, many of which are meant for laboratory animals, large animals, etc. and so will not be included here. There are three types of euthanasia: inhalant administration, non-inhalant pharmaceutical agent administration, and physical methods. To be frank, the guidelines do not list two of my techniques as acceptable methods of euthanasia; these being the intrahepatic and intrarenal injections. The way the guidelines are worded indicates that they are not acceptable methods under any circumstance. However, after speaking with the AVMA's animal welfare committee, it is clear that they are acceptable when performed under heavy sedation or anesthesia. In fact, almost any method of euthanasia is acceptable if the pet is unaware, pain free, and unable to regain consciousness. My reasons for using these techniques stem from the presence of the owners and the need for more rapid drug uptake than a standard intraperitoneal injection would allow. The new guidelines, currently being updated in 2010, will include information about new acceptable techniques like these. Intrahepatic and intrarenal injections are already widely used in veterinary practices around the world.

I will share with you my preferred techniques, but you may know of others that also work well. Hopefully, what I have written complements what you already know and will provide you with some tips and pointers to make your protocol even better.

The method of euthanasia you choose will depend on many things:

1. Your comfort with the technique
2. Your supplies
3. The presence of onlookers
4. The type of euthanasia solution you use and amount you have available
5. The signalment and physical condition of the pet
6. The need for a postmortem exam

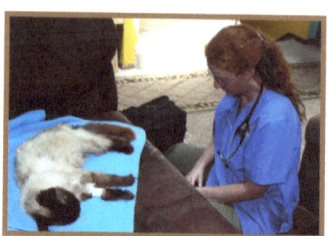

1. Your comfort with the technique

When you have experience with a particular technique, you know what to expect and how to handle the situation if something unexpected happens. But don't limit yourself. You should know at least two other methods in case circumstances force you to abandon your preferred technique.

2. Your supplies

As you prepare your supplies, make sure to include things that you use for your standard euthanasia techniques as well as emergency equipment. For example, I prefer placing catheters for intravenous injections. My bag is stocked with two different sizes of catheters to fit the size of my patient, and I carry a lot of catheters with me in case I have difficulties getting good venous access. If I find that I need to give an intracardiac injection instead of using a vein, I reach for the 1.5 inch long needles that I always carry with me.

3. The presence of onlookers

This is important. Veterinarians know that as long as a pet is sedated or unconscious, most methods of euthanasia are humane. As long as death is painless and relatively quick, any of the approved methods are acceptable. I say relatively quick because intraperitoneal injections take longer, but are still very humane and easy on the pet. However, when family members are watching, you should pick the least shocking technique available, such as an intravenous injection. Most clients expect euthanasia to be done via a vein, and when you do something different, they may be hesitant to accept it.

I helped a pug one time that had very poor veins. The owner was a young teenager, and she held the pug on her lap during the entire appointment. I could see right away that venous access was going to be an issue, but I tried to place a catheter anyway, just because I knew it would be easier on the family. When it became clear that placing a catheter was impossible, I told everyone present that I was going to give the "medicine" gently into her belly and that she would pass very peacefully. The pug was deeply sedated already and to me, choosing this method was a non-issue. The family was quite taken aback. The mother asked me why, if this method was so good, I didn't start with that first. Her vet had always used intravenous injections and she felt that was the best way. I told her that most people expect intravenous euthanasia and that was why I started in that manner, but I moved onto something that would work better for her daughter's pug under these circumstances. Even after more explanation and the pug passing peacefully and quickly, I still don't think they believed that this was an acceptable euthanasia technique. My point is that even if you know a particular method works well, make sure the family is on board and fully understands the reasoning and benefits of one method over another. If you sense that they are unsure, address their concerns and then move on to accomplish a peaceful euthanasia.

Many vets prefer intracardiac injections and will perform them on every pet, regardless of the situation. When the family is present, they might drape the chest area to block the family's view, similar to when a woman has a Caesarean birth. I also know vets who will refuse to do an intracardiac injection when the family is present. My personal feeling is that if the family fully understands what is going to happen and wants to be present, let them. Let them witness whatever they feel they can handle.

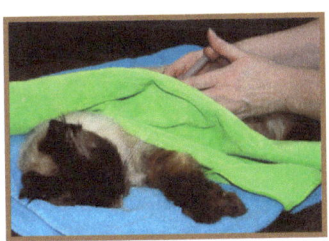

4. The type of euthanasia solution you use and the amount you have available.

Most of you will be using a barbiturate solution to achieve euthanasia. All of them are highly alkaline and natremic, which according to a recent paper, raises the question of tissue irritation. This being said, certain euthanasia solutions are more irritating than others, which is why some are approved for only intravenous use. When these irritating solutions come in contact with tissue outside of a vein, an awake animal will usually react.

> *A few years ago, I attempted to euthanize a dog using a catheter placed by a local clinic. When the dog was sedated, I flushed it with saline and everything appeared normal. I placed an extension set to give the family some room and started to inject. When the solution made its way up to the catheter tip, the dog sat straight up and screamed. Everyone gasped and my heart sank. I calmly told the family that the original catheter wasn't going to work and I placed another one so we could proceed. After the dog died, I removed the old catheter and saw that it was still within the vein. During her stay in the clinic, this dog had chewed on her catheters and the technicians had to place braces on her legs to keep them in place. I suspect that this dog's veins were traumatized, and the solution contacted an area of phlebitis. Whatever the cause, this dog's discomfort was significant enough to override her heavy sedation. This was an extremely rare case, but it proves the point that most euthanasia solutions are irritating.*

Keep in mind that if you are giving an intravenous injection to an unsedated animal and the vein blows, it will be painful regardless of what you are injecting. Even nonirritating solutions or extravasated blood is painful due to the distension of the surrounding fascia. We need to give credit to all the animals that quietly tolerate our failed attempts at venipuncture.

If you choose to administer euthanasia solution into the heart, liver, or kidney, sedation is mandatory. In the shelter setting, euthanasia agents are routinely injected via intraperitoneal injections in awake animals. This is approved because shelter personnel use what are currently considered to be non-irritating euthanasia agents and they avoid injecting into abdominal organs. Should research show that even this technique is painful, shelters will have to adopt inexpensive pre-sedation protocols for all animals undergoing intraperitoneal injections.

The amount of solution you have on hand is also important when choosing your technique. The standard dose for nearly all euthanasia solutions is 1 ml per 10 pounds of body weight. For example, a 50-pound dog needs to receive at least 5 mls of euthanasia solution to bring about cardiac arrest. When euthanasia drugs are created, this is the standard used in their formulation, which makes life easier for veterinarians. The recommended doses work very well for intravenous and intracardiac injections, as long as the amount you give goes where it needs to go. When performing an intraperitoneal injection, give at least three times the traditional dose due to the slower uptake time and the risk of "third-spacing." If you find yourself with only a small amount of euthanasia solution, choose a technique that requires the smallest volume possible, such as an intravenous injection. Intracardiac injections can be tricky, especially if you have a hard time locating the heart and the solution ends up in the lungs or pleural space. If you do not have enough solution, you may find yourself unable to complete euthanasia.

5. The signalment and physical condition of the pet

The signalment and physical condition of the animal you are helping should always be a factor when choosing your euthanasia technique. Weight, size, disease, species, and even breed all contribute to how well a particular technique can be expected to work.

* **Weight** – The only time I consider weight to be an issue is in the case of obese animals. Obesity makes veins harder to see and feel, makes the chest wall thicker, creates large amounts of intraabdominal fat, and leads to increased dyspnea during sedation. If my patient is an overweight cat, I will choose an intravenous rather than an intrarenal injection because finding and isolating a kidney could be difficult. If my patient is an overweight Dachshund, I find placing a catheter in the front leg to be much easier than in a rear leg and so on.

* **Age** – Age by itself does not affect your technique. What would is all the changes the body has gone through during the animal's life. The dog may have lost a leg at age five thus making you choose a different leg for intravenous injection, one you may not normally use. You can also assume that the older pet will be weaker, have an underlying disease of some sort, and thus you need to tailor your methods accordingly.

* **Disease** –The presence of illness, be it heart disease, cancer, renal failure, etc., can affect blood pressure, circulation, perfusion, and drug uptake. If your patient has extremely low blood pressure and the veins are flat, consider an intracardiac or intraperitoneal injection. If the heart wall is thickened, or is surrounded by a tumor or a hemopericardium, you may want to avoid an intracardiac injection. If peripheral edema is present, veins may be virtually impossible to find. When this happens, you may need to abandon an intravenous injection altogether. If a dog has ascites or a hemoabdomen, an intraperitoneal injection would not be the best choice, and so on.

Another factor to consider is how well your patient will tolerate sedation. If your patient is having a hard time breathing, choose a technique that allows you to proceed very quickly in case his dyspnea worsens. It is hard to watch a dog struggle to breathe while waiting for an intraperitoneal injection to stop the heart.

* **Species** – For our purposes, we are talking only about dogs, cats, and exotics like pocket pets, reptiles, and medium to small birds. In most cases, dogs and cats are euthanized easily by intravenous, intracardiac, or intraabdominal injections. Exotics however are a bit more difficult. I know many doctors who do not feel comfortable euthanizing exotics because of all the variables they present: scales, feathers, shells, varying drug uptake rates, etc. My preferred method of exotic animal euthanasia is by intraperitoneal injection. They are sedated first with IM Telazol® and acepromazine and when they show no response to stimuli, I inject 6 mls of euthanasia solution into the abdomen, regardless of their size and weight.

***Breeds** – Different breeds can vary wildly in their physical and physiological attributes. A long-legged breed is easier to catheterize than a short-legged breed. One characteristic that I find challenging is the brachycephalic head. These dogs and cats have a tendency to become dyspneic under sedation and also may overheat when outdoors or lying in front of the fire. Thick or thin-coated breeds may have similar problems with environmental conditions. Some breeds are prone to heart disease while others typically suffer

from kidney disease, which might influence your choice of euthanasia technique. My least favorite breed to euthanize is the Pekingese. They are brachycephalic, short-legged, have tiny hearts, and often suffer from heart disease making every detail of the euthanasia process a challenge.

6. The need for a postmortem exam

It is important to know whether or not an animal will be studied following euthanasia. If so, choose a technique that minimizes organ and tissue damage. The solution itself will circulate throughout the body and cause changes, but you can avoid injecting near or into an organ of special interest. If I know that my feline patient is going to be part of a study on renal disease, I am not going to inject a kidney. Laboratory researchers have a variety of euthanasia techniques that general practitioners do not use in private practice, because of their need to preserve tissues. For a description of these other methods, see the AVMA euthanasia guidelines.

Routes of Administration

1. Intravenous Injection

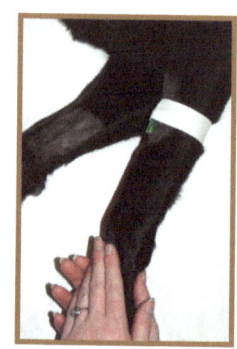

Pros – Fast and effective
Standard dosing of euthanasia solution
Sedation not required

Cons – Venous access necessary
Blood pressure concerns
Requires moderate skill

In order to perform an intravenous injection, you need to find a vein to work with. The accessory cephalic and cephalic veins in the front leg and the medial and lateral saphenous veins in the back leg are easy to see and feel. Each has its pros and cons, which I've gone into in the catheter placement chapter. Pick the one that is most appropriate under the circumstances. I will attempt to place a catheter in any dog over 5 pounds before resorting to another method. Even very small dogs can have outstanding leg veins.

The veins themselves will be covered with the skin and usually lie on top of or in the grooves between neighboring muscles, tendons, and ligaments. The lower on the limb you are, the more "roly-poly" veins become. The more proximal you move, the more stable they become. When choosing your catheter site, look out for skin diseases, masses, etc. that will make placement difficult.

Prepare your solution ahead of time if you can. My service administers the standard dose of 1 ml per 10 pounds, but we then add an extra 2 mls to be on the safe side. For a dog weighing 65 pounds, we will round up to 70 pounds and give 7 mls plus 2 mls for a total of 9 mls. This is especially important because we often do not have the dog's exact weight. It also helps to have some extra euthanasia solution in your syringe if some of the drug leaks from your catheter set up, such as when a luer lock is not securely fastened. You should give no less than 1 ml of euthanasia solution to any pet. If your euthanasia solution is extremely thick, you can dilute it with saline to ease its movement through the needle and catheter. The saline does not negatively affect cardiac arrest time or postmortem side effects. If you insert your euthanasia syringe with needle directly into the vein, make sure to draw back and check for blood. To be safe, you should draw back at least once during venous administration to make sure that your needle is still placed correctly.

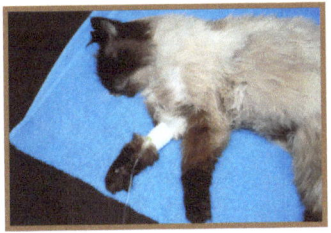 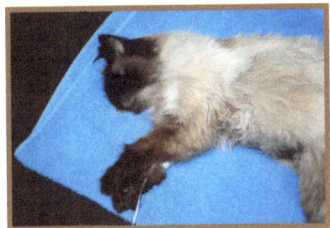

An example of covering your IV catheter placement from view

Once you have your needle inserted directly into the vein or a catheter placed, inject slowly and steadily to avoid putting too much pressure on your set up. When all of the solution has been injected, and you are certain it all went into the vein, you can remove your needle. Apply pressure to your injection site to stop any bleeding. If you have a catheter placed, you can flush with saline to clear your catheter of the last of the euthanasia solution. When performing an intravenous injection, remember that death occurs very quickly. You should start to see the effects of your injection within 30 seconds or so. Let the family know what they might see before you start injecting. In the next section, we will go over what to expect around the time of death in greater detail. Once death has occurred, remove the catheter and wipe your injection site with the hydrogen peroxide-soaked gauze.

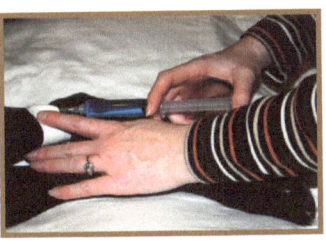 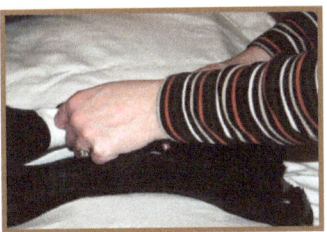

Try to hide your euthanasia injection from view

As I mentioned in the catheter placement chapter, if you see a bleb forming in the surrounding tissue, you have slipped out of the vein. If the pet is fully sedated, you should not see any reaction. Try to inject again higher up the leg. If that doesn't work, move to another vein and try again. In the worst-case scenario of not being able to access a vein in another leg, you will need to switch to an intracardiac or intraabdominal injection. My preference would be an intraperitoneal/intrahepatic injection if the dog is less than 20 pounds or an intracardiac injection if the dog is bigger.

2. Intracardiac Injection

Pros – Fast and effective
 Eliminates venous pressure concerns
 Works for almost every domesticated pet

Cons – General perception as gruesome
 Requires advanced skill
 Requires sedation

Intracardiac injections have been performed by veterinary practitioners for a very long time. We do cardiac sticks for a variety of reasons, most often when veins are not accessible or when an immediate death with little to no preparation is desirable, such as with a seizuring dog. However, no studies have ever been conducted, except for maybe one on opossums, comparing this method to other euthanasia techniques or to determine what depth of sedation is necessary for an animal to be completely pain free. The trick is to perform the procedure accurately, and when the family is present, doing it with finesse and grace.

The easiest way to give an intracardiac injection is to have the pet lying in lateral recumbency on either their right or left side. I prefer to have a dog lying on its right side because the heart is easier to auscult from the left and the left ventricle is usually the easiest chamber to hit. The left side of the chest also has fewer lung lobes, but the right side does have the cardiac notch where no lung tissue resides. Be prepared for heart and lung disease to complicate things – thickened myocardium, tumors, displacement, pulmonary edema/effusion, or even a large lipoma over the chest wall can make an intracardiac injection difficult.

According to Pasquini's *Anatomy of Domestic Animals*, the heart in most dogs and cats will reside from the 2nd or 3rd intercostal space (ICS) to the 5th or 6th ICS and from the sternum to about two-thirds of the way up the thorax. In my experience, the heart is usually more cranial and ventral than I think it will be. When ausculting the heart, you need to pinpoint the PMI or Point of Maximum Intensity. On the left side of the chest, this will likely be the point of the aortic valve located in the 4th intercostal space or the mitral valve in the 5th intercostal space. On the right side, the right AV valve will be the loudest and is also in the 4th intercostal space at the level of the olecranon/elbow. The olecranon is located near the 5th intercostal space so there will be little heart caudal to this point. Use your stethoscope or even your hand to find the Point of Maximum intensity (PMI) on the chest wall. Then, grasp the lower antebrachium and press the elbow up the chest wall to simulate where it would normally be if the pet were standing. A good place to insert your needle is usually just a bit cranial to the point of the elbow. Combining the location of the PMI with this landmark should help you find the heart.

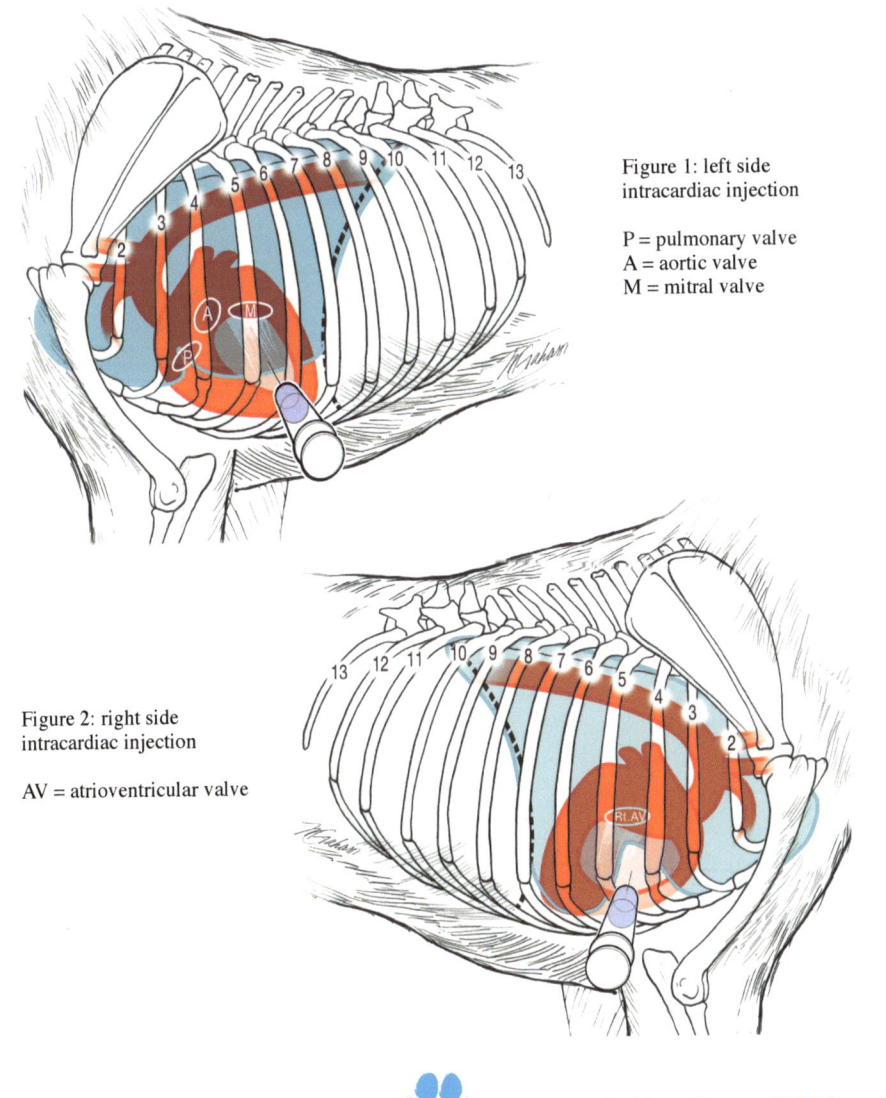

Figure 1: left side intracardiac injection

P = pulmonary valve
A = aortic valve
M = mitral valve

Figure 2: right side intracardiac injection

AV = atrioventricular valve

In-Home Pet Euthanasia Techniques

If you are using a cardiac injection as your euthanasia technique, make sure everything is ready to go before you even locate the injection site. Your patient must be unconscious. He should not react in any way to your injection.

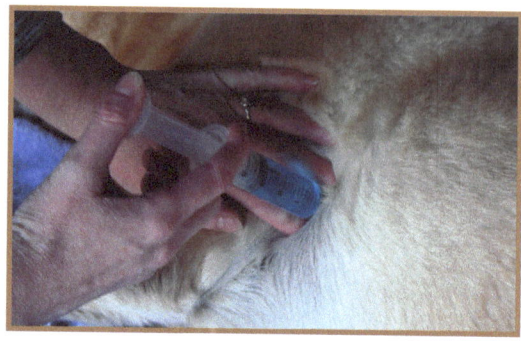

Make sure you draw up enough euthanasia solution to stop the heart because you don't want to have to inject a second time unless absolutely necessary. If your canine patient weighs 40 pounds, draw up at least 6 mls. This way you have a little extra to spare in case you accidentally inject some outside of the heart. Use a larger syringe than is necessary to hold the solution. When injecting into the heart, you have to draw back blood to make sure you are within a chamber and therefore you need a little extra room in your syringe. If giving 6 mls of solution, I will use a 12 ml syringe. If there is pulmonary effusion present, you might miss the heart on your first stick and accidentally draw up some of the fluid. If you have extra room in the syringe, you can gently redirect and try again without having to draw up a new syringe full of euthanasia solution. If you find yourself within an airway, you will draw back air, and again it is nice to have a little extra space available in your syringe.

When performing an intracardiac injection in larger dogs, you will need to use a long needle. My service uses 1.5" to 2" 18 gauge needles for dogs over 30 pounds. As you prepare to enter the chest wall, keep your needle perpendicular to the body. Angling the needle will increase the distance you need to travel before hitting the heart. If you contact a rib during penetration of the chest wall, either start over or gently walk your needle tip off the rib edge and keep going. When you think you are in the heart, draw back on the plunger. If you draw back and get negative pressure, your needle tip is within something solid (e.g., the myocardium, a tumor, etc.). Push the needle in farther if you can and try to draw back again. If you still do not aspirate blood, gently redirect and try again, without removing the needle completely from the chest. The only time I pull out completely is if I need to draw up more solution. Remember that if you let go of a syringe that is inserted into the heart, it may move along with the contractions. This is disturbing for families to see so try to avoid doing so if possible. Use your free hand to shield the syringe from view. On more than one occasion I have had owners tell me they never even noticed when I gave the injection. You may also want to put up a drape of some sort to help limit visibility.

Once you see blood in your syringe, you are free to administer your solution. It is always good practice to draw back again halfway through your injection just to make sure you are still in the heart. Sometimes we might push too hard or the pet's breathing lifts our needle out of a chamber. Once you get very comfortable with the technique, you probably don't have to do this. When all of the solution has entered the heart, death should occur quickly.

If you are having a hard time locating the heart, and your syringe is now full of fluid (both solution and pulmonary fluid) or air, gently express your syringe into the chest so that the family's eyes aren't drawn to the mixture, remove your needle, and quickly reload to try again. If you don't feel comfortable doing this, express your syringe into your trash container and redraw fresh solution. Remember, your patient should be completely asleep at this point and injecting a small amount of euthanasia solution into the chest should not have any adverse effects. I have never seen an animal become dyspneic or struggle when this is done.

In the rare instance when you feel you have located the heart, have seen blood in your syringe, and injected successfully only to find that the pet is not passing, you have likely injected your solution into a hemopericardium or have "third spaced" somewhere. Your solution is trapped and is not making its way to the brainstem. At this point you can try another cardiac injection or move to another location like the liver.

When considering an intracardiac injection, let the family know why you feel this method is best for their pet. Many families have shared with me their frustration and anxiety over seeing another pet have their heart injected. They found it very hard to watch and accept. I don't know whether the vet failed to fully explain the situation, but I hear this time and time again. My service uses cardiac injections only in special cases when no other method is appropriate, and we make sure the client is on board with us before proceeding.

3. Intraperitoneal Injection

Pros – Easy to perform
Works in all domesticated pets

Cons – Longer time to absorb
More solution needed
Possible to accidentally inject organs
Sedation ideal

Intraperitoneal injections are very common and work on all domesticated pets. Shelters in particular use this technique on a daily basis due to the low level of skill required to perform them and the lack of a requirement for sedation. An intraperitoneal injection means that the euthanasia solution is given into the peritoneal space (i.e., the abdomen.) The solution must therefore miss neighboring organs or the administration would be considered intraorgan, and without sedation, is considered painful. Even though pre-sedation is not required for this technique, I ALWAYS give it. If you are concerned about IP injection pain and cannot presedate, I recommend you use FP-3® once it is back on the market.

Shelter personnel teach this technique extensively to their euthanasia staff. According the HSUS Euthanasia Training Manual, the two areas for injection are the ventral midline caudal to the umbilicus or low on the right lateral abdomen. The needle should be inserted at an angle slightly toward the head and the syringe plunger pulled to aspirate for negative pressure or air. If no blood or fluid is seen in the syringe, you are free to inject. Because the euthanasia solution is moving into the blood stream through absorption across abdominal organ membranes and serosal linings, it may take longer to achieve cardiac death. If your patient is still alive after 20-30 minutes, I would personally give more solution. When necessary, massage the abdomen to help the solution absorb. This technique is best in small pets and should be avoided in large dogs.

In the home setting with family gathered close, waiting even 10 minutes for an intraperitoneal injection to work is going to be stressful for everyone. I recommend giving 3 times the normal dose of your euthanasia solution to speed the uptake rate. If you have to give more than one injection, do so subtly and make sure the family knows that things are progressing as you expect them to. Once you have given your total amount, sit back and allow the drug to do its work. Intraperitoneal injections take more time, but this time is peaceful and easy for the pet. Remind the family that their sweetheart is working deeper and deeper into their sleep and will soon pass away.

All of my exotic pet euthanasias are done via intraperitoneal injections. They are presedated with Telazol® and acepromazine IM or SQ and then 6 ml euthanasia solution is administered using a 1 inch 22 gauge needle along the ventral midline. Because most of these pets are very small, they pass within 3-5 minutes at most.

4. Intrahepatic Injection

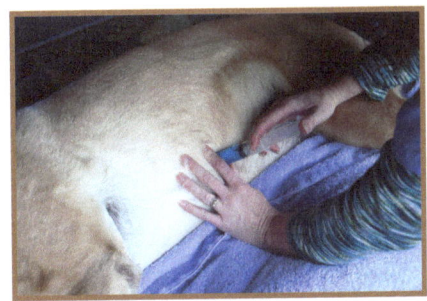

Pros – Simple technique
Works well when other techniques fail
Works in almost every domesticated pet

Cons – Requires sedation
More solution needed

The liver is large, highly vascular, and usually easy to palpate. Veterinarians choose intrahepatic injections over intraperitoneal injections because of the improved uptake of euthanasia solution. This organ resides right up against the diaphragm and for the most part, takes up to half of the caudal rib cage space. Seated within its curvature will be the stomach, gall bladder, and proximal small intestine. When an intravenous injection is not viable, an intrahepatic injection can be a great alternative.

Like intracardiac injections, intrahepatic injections need to be done under complete sedation. They cause pain in a conscious animal due to parenchymal swelling and possible irritation from the euthanasia solution. Before injecting the liver, make sure the pet is completely asleep – pinch the toes to assess deep pain, touch around the eye, etc. When no response is seen, it is safe to proceed. Take a few moments to explain what you are doing so the family can understand what to expect. Let them know that their pet may pass immediately or within just a few minutes and that you will listen to the heart to confirm the death.

Choose a needle length that is sufficient for reaching the liver. With small pets, a 1-inch needle should be adequate, but in larger pets, a 1.5" or 2" needle may be necessary. I also recommend giving more euthanasia solution than you would use for an intravenous euthanasia. I generally double the dose because the rate of absorption can be delayed based on how well you place your injection. There is no specific research on this dose that I have found. If you miss the liver with a standard dose, death may not occur in a reasonable amount of time so having more solution present will help speed things along.

To inject the liver, place your needle in the notch on either side of the xyphoid process and aim cranially, up under the last rib of your laterally recumbent pet. You can even apply some inward pressure with the syringe or with your free hand to allow the needle to move deeper. If you have palpated the liver anywhere dorsal to the xyphoid process, inject where you feel is most appropriate. There is no need to draw back and check for blood. Keep the needle in the ventral half of the abdomen to avoid the stomach, which is located more dorsally. I like intrahepatic injections because they work well from either the left or right side.

I would like to say that all appointments run smoothly, but in reality they just can't. Sometimes the most straightforward case becomes challenging. I was called out to help a female Chow with chronic pyometra. She was a breeding bitch and the owners did not want to spay her or continue with treatment. She was in good weight and still relatively young at seven years of age, but without treatment, she was going to suffer and euthanasia was warranted. Now I have helped many Chows in the past and there are two things about them that set them apart from other breeds. The first is that they seem to take longer to sedate and the second is their thick skin. One-person catheter placement can be very difficult with a Chow, which is exactly what happened with her.

I gave her the sedative and after fifteen minutes, she lay down and relaxed. Once it worked into her system, she went to sleep very quickly and even started to snore. Her owners were very comfortable with everything and trusted I would proceed with things as I needed too. That turned out to be very important because for the next 10 minutes, I worked to find a vein. As usual, I started with the lateral saphenous vein of her left rear leg. Not only did I not find a vein, I saw no blood, not even a drop from her catheter insertion site. I tried three times on that leg and nothing changed. Next I moved to her left cephalic vein and again, the same situation. Three times I tried to place the catheter and no blood was seen, not even a SQ bleb. Her owner was more than gracious and understanding. She even apologized for her dog using up so many catheters.

So rather than continuing on this path, I decided to do a gentle cardiac injection. She was still snoring away and unaware of anything. I switched to my inch and a half long needles, located my best point, and inserted the needle. Much to my dismay, still no blood. I tried again and nothing. At this, I looked at the owner and she smiled. "I guess you see it all" she said. "A dog with no blood must be one in a million." Thank heavens for this owner's patience. I went ahead and gave a double dose of euthanasia solution up towards the liver and she died immediately. I was so relieved.

At the time of this appointment, I had helped over 1500 pets pass peacefully at home. When I think of technically challenging euthanasias, she is the first to come to mind.

Death should occur within about two minutes or so with a well-performed intrahepatic injection, but I usually tell families that their friend may pass immediately or it may take a few minutes. Either situation is perfectly normal. Breathing should stop almost immediately. If you give your double-dose injection and breathing continues, you can give another dose right away aiming for another point in the liver. I like to tell the family that "I'm just going to give the rest now." Most people are not familiar with intraabdominal injections and will not think it strange that you are giving more solution. Keep everything flowing smoothly for the family. If you give the second injection and the pet continues to breathe, just gently massage the region and ask the family to tell a story about their pet or sit quietly. Remember you have already prepared the family that it may take a few minutes. If euthanasia takes longer than 10 minutes, you have performed an intraperitoneal injection, which is fine, but cardiac death will take longer. Again, let the family know that their pet is experiencing a peaceful albeit slower passing.

Once you see the pet stop breathing, gently place your hand over the heart to feel for a beat. If the heart is still beating, continue your abdominal massage a bit longer and then feel again before listening with your stethoscope. Do not be afraid to give even more solution if you feel things are taking too long. Families are all different; some cannot stand waiting more than 5 minutes for death to occur while others will be content for much longer. Watch their body language, listen to their comments, and give more solution if you need. You can explain the slow passing by talking about low blood pressures, poor perfusion, abdominal fat, etc. When possible, do not let things continue longer than what the family is comfortable with. The pet will not care if you give another injection since he is sleeping.

5. Intrarenal Injections

Pros –   Great for cats and small mammals
         Fast and effective

Cons –   Requires sedation
         Requires moderate skill

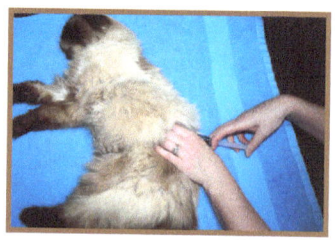

In my practice, we reserve intrarenal injections for cats and small mammals and they have been a wonderful addition to my euthanasia service. This method is a great choice if venous access is difficult or when preparing a catheter site is too obtrusive. As with intrahepatic injections, the kidneys will speed the rate of absorption over standard intraperitoneal injections. Like with all intraorgan injections, patients must not feel the injection so complete sedation is required. I will use cats as my example in describing how to perform an intrarenal injection.

Feline kidneys are usually easy to palpate, especially if your patient is older or has lost some weight, but you should be able to feel them even in overweight cats. They are just a little harder to isolate. The right kidney resides more cranially than does the left. It is usually located just under the last 2 ribs along the dorsum. It is contained within the retroperitoneal space and is therefore harder to manipulate. The left kidney in contrast is more caudal, not covered by the ribs, and is within peritoneal space. The left kidney in most cats is easy to find and manipulate.

When choosing which kidney to inject, pick the one that you can feel and isolate the best. For me, this is almost always the left one. You should be able to grasp it easily and curl your fingers under it. If a cat is in renal failure, the kidneys may be smaller, have a nodular feeling, or even be impossible to locate. If you have doubts about one kidney, consider using the other. Also make sure that you are not palpating a fecal ball in the colon. If you are using the right kidney, you may have to use your forefinger to manipulate it into reach. Gently push your finger up under the last rib to find it and move it caudally. It will only shift by a centimeter or two. Once your feline patient is deeply asleep and you are prepared for an intrarenal injection, you can let the owner hold the cat on his or her lap or you can place the cat on any flat surface.

For left kidney injections, lay the cat on its right side with feet toward the owner while you sit behind its back. Owners like this because they can look into their cat's face. In essence, you will have the cat positioned between you and the owner with the cat facing them. Gently run your hands along the abdomen to find the kidney and feel for any abdominal muscle tensing. If the cat tenses, it is not sedated enough for you to proceed. If necessary, give more sedation until no response is noted. When you are ready to inject, use your right hand to push the kidney upward, from the cat's downside, into your left hand and cup the left kidney under your fingertips raising it up parallel with the spine. If you have a hard time doing this, just hold it firmly in position and don't let it slip out of your grasp. You want to keep ahold of the kidney through your entire injection. If you accidentally let go in mid-injection, try to hold it in place within the abdomen using your fingers and finish the injection. If you cannot find the kidney again, gently advance the syringe toward the liver and finish injecting. If you want to inject into the right kidney, simply lay the cat on its left side and use the same technique This being said, you might be able to isolate the right kidney with the cat laying on his right side and in these cases turning the cat is unnecessary.

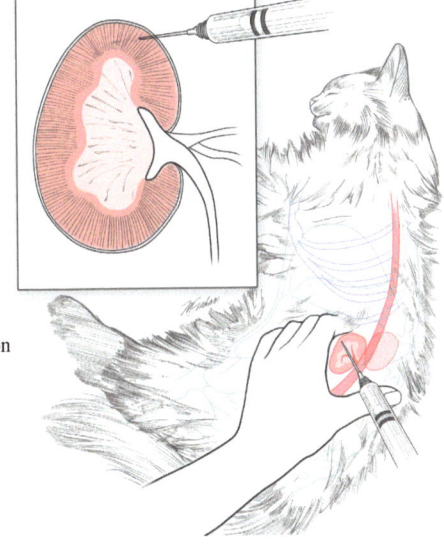

Figure 3:

Left intrarenal injection

When you insert the needle, hold your syringe close to the body. You can even shield your syringe from view by tucking it below the hand holding the kidney. This is a very effective way to hide the injection from the family. If the kidney is located deep in the abdomen, but you can still feel it, you will have to hold your syringe perpendicular to the body. This is not as subtle, but it works.

As is the case with intrahepatic injections, you need to give more solution than an intravenous injection would require. My service has a standard protocol of 6 mls per renal injection in a cat of any size. This helps ensure euthanasia takes place quickly and standardizes our drug record keeping.

Upon injection, you should feel the kidney swell in your fingers. This is a good indication that you are positioned properly within the kidney's cortex. The renal cortex is highly vascular and your euthanasia solution should be quickly taken up into the renal vein. During injection, you may feel the renal capsule "pop." This is normal and indicates the solution is infiltrating the cortex correctly. I have no true scientific proof of this, but I have performed one post mortem exam on a kidney with a popped capsule and it was the cortex that was injected. Continue to inject all of your solution. If you are certain you are positioned correctly and the kidney does not swell, you might be injecting into the renal pelvis, which may slow absorption. Kidney swelling does not guarantee immediate death, but it does increase the odds that death will occur faster. Either way, watch the cat for cessation of breathing. Most of the time, your feline patient will stop breathing even before you finish the injection. As with intrahepatic injections, let the family know ahead of time that their cat may pass immediately or within just a few minutes. That way they are prepared whatever happens.

If you have given the contents of the whole syringe and your feline patient is still breathing normally, draw up another 6 mls and tell the family that you will now "give the rest." You can use the same kidney again or inject into the liver. I never give more than two injections to a cat and I never turn the cat over to inject the other kidney. There really is no need. The second injection should cause respiratory arrest if not immediate death. If you need to wait a few minutes, just rub the belly gently and ask the family a few questions about their pet's life. I like to gently place my hand over the heart to feel for a heartbeat before I listen with my stethoscope. When all is quiet, let everyone know the heart has stopped beating.

In-Home Pet Euthanasia Techniques

With any of these techniques, take your time and be consistent. I have not listed every euthanasia technique here, only those that you will use on a regular basis in the home. If you feel the method that you start out with is not going to work, readily move on to another to ensure things continue smoothly for the family and the pet. I also encourage you to learn as much about different techniques as you can, even those used on species that you don't normally work on. You never know when you might get a call to help a horse, a cow, or pot-bellied pig.

Time to Grieve

Tips on helping families begin the mourning process

Most veterinarians have not had a lot of training in how to deal with grief and loss. Our understanding of these situations usually comes more from life experience. In our roles as care providers, it is imperative that we strive to learn all we can to support our clients on their journey through grief. Helping families begin a healthy mourning process begins during the appointment itself. Being at home provides them with safety to grieve and open up.

If you haven't done so already, take some time to learn what you should and should not do or say to a grieving client. Pet loss companioning courses are available around the country, and dozens of books have been written to help us recognize what our clients are trying to say and to teach us ways to help them move forward as well as reflect on their loss. *Companioning the Bereaved* by Dr. Alan Wolfelt is a wonderful book designed to teach us how to partner and communicate with people experiencing an unthinkable loss. Listed here are some key concepts shared in Alan's book. If you can follow these concepts during your time with a grieving family, you will be a trusted companion on their journey towards healing.

Be comfortable with silence

It is important to offer quiet time. When you can, provide a peaceful setting for the family. People become more confused and disoriented when they are bombarded with outside noise. The quiet can be comforting. Following euthanasia, pronounce the pet deceased, then step out of the room and give families space to acknowledge the death of their pet. This is commonly done in the clinic setting and translates well into the home. Quietly excuse yourself and let them know you will be back in a few minutes. Step outside or into another room until you feel they are ready to move forward. When you come back into the room, let them talk first. Depending on the family, they might want a few minutes by themselves, or perhaps they would prefer that you stay. A client once told me that what she remembered most about me was my willingness to sit in silence with her. They will let you know if time alone is too difficult.

If there are other people in the room who are making noise or talking about random topics in an effort to "cheer up" their friend, ask your client if they would like some quiet time as a cue for the others to step out with you. Well-meaning family and friends who are uncomfortable with silence often talk incessantly. I find they often talk about their own losses. While I realize this is important for them, especially when the present loss may bring up sad memories, it is not what your client needs. Under these circumstances, I offer my sympathies to the person doing the talking and bring the focus back to my client and the pet.

Silence in the middle of a conversation is very important also. Don't be afraid of those long pregnant pauses. If you are a rapid talker, figure out some way to slow yourself down. I like to take deep slow breaths throughout the appointment and relax my body. Let the family, and not you, fill the quiet times with anything that they want to say. Remember the saying "Mouth closed, ears open, and presence available."

Acknowledge their relief

It is so hard to watch a loved one suffer. When death finally comes, your client might feel instant relief. Relief does not equal a lack of love; it is just a response to the end of suffering. Anticipatory grief is very demanding on the body and soul. When it is over, it is natural to feel release. When my own dog died in 2010, my mind was happy she was free, but my heart ached. If you see that your client is feeling relief, acknowledge it as healthy and normal.

Honor the power of crying

Crying is one way of showing our emotional pain. It is a cleansing, soulful thing. It never ceases to amaze me how someone can seem so calm and collected before death, but the moment I pronounce their pet deceased, the tears pour out of them. I am truly honored when someone feels safe enough to cry in my presence. If I see them struggle with it, I remind them that we all want someone to cry for us. Make sure there are tissues close by.

It is always acceptable for us, the veterinarians caring for pets at a time of great need, to cry as well. The family will be honored that you have felt a strong connection with them and the human-animal bond they shared with their pet. It is important, however, that your emotions do not overshadow those of the grieving family.

Be a stable person for them

The time immediately following the death of their pet is critical for owners. They can feel disorientated, confused, scared, angry, and much more. Whatever their emotions, pattern your behavior appropriately so that you can assist them. If they are shaking, offer a gentle hand on their shoulder. If they are talking incessantly, just sit and listen. If they curl up on the floor with their dog, direct other people out of the room to give them space.

During this time, you can guide clients toward making final preparations. Offer some details about what you are doing and take away any guesswork. Rather than just leaning down and making the paw print, tell them "I'm going to make her paw print now. You can stay right where you are." Or "I'm going to take my things out to the car and when I come back, we will wrap her in a blanket and carry her out." Families may not be thinking clearly, and you need to make sure they understand what is happening.

If the owner is expressing negative emotions, try to be tolerant and do not pass judgment. You will help calm them by staying quietly passive and patient. Remember that anger is a stage of grief, and it might be directed at you. If they have a legitimate reason to be upset, for instance if the euthanasia was technically challenging, take it in stride and move on. If a client is still angry when you leave, either because of their grief or frustration with you, call them in a week or so and see how they are doing.

Guilt is a normal response to loss

Grief is so painful that most people will avoid it at all cost. This is why so many of our animal patients are obviously suffering by the time we arrive. Families don't want to face the loss. Later, they often tell me they feel guilt about letting their pet suffer for so long. They feel guilt for not taking them on enough walks, for feeding too much human food, for living in a house with too many stairs, for focusing on their kids more than the pets, etc. As caring people, we are tempted to explain away their guilt, to rationalize it for them. But, as Dr. Wolfelt puts it, only by exploring what they should and should not feel guilty about does the mourner come to some understanding of the limits of their responsibility. Our role as the veterinarian is to be supportive and non-judgmental. Thank the family for being so wonderful to their pet and praise them for the strength they found to say goodbye.

We cannot "fix" their pain

Most people in an owner's life do not fully understand the depth of the loss and pain that they face when their pet dies. It is the client's right to mourn, to feel awful, and to get away for a while. Just as we cannot take away the guilt, we cannot take away their pain and sadness. Statements like "It was for the best" or "You'll feel better tomorrow" only complicate things. The pain of the loss remains even when they know their pet's suffering is over. One of my favorite sayings, "The only way to end her suffering was to make yours begin" is in direct acknowledgement of the pain they are taking on.

I encourage you to learn about empathy statements and the power they have. Statements like "This must be very hard for you." "It's a very helpless feeling isn't it." and "She was your best friend wasn't she" are priceless to the person hearing them. Empathy statements will help you slow down your appointments and focus in on the family you are there to support. They are said to understand the pain, not fix it.

Honor the power of ceremony

Home euthanasia allows families the freedom to express themselves in a way the clinic cannot. Ceremonies are a beautiful way to honor pets and the family members who loved them. They can be as simple as reading a poem or releasing a memorial balloon to more elaborate settings like a funeral. Ceremonies allow the family to share their pain and joys with loved ones in their life. They mark the transition from life with the pet to without.

You can offer to arrange for a ceremony as part of your service or simply help families think about what they might want before you arrive. It is all a part of making preparations. There is a nation-wide trend towards offering pet loss ceremonies and now might be the time to look into what you can provide in your area.

Here are a few examples of prayers and meditations that you can offer during a service:

Loving creator of all that is, we turn to you in prayer at this time of remembrance. The link of life that bound us to _____ has been broken, but feelings of love continue to bind us together.

We give thanks for the gift of _____ life, companionship, and memory. Help us understand how our lives have been formed and shaped by what _____ was and did.

May his/her memory be a blessing. As long as we live, _____ too will live, for they are part of us as long as we remember them.

May I find the strength to mourn with dignity.

May I find the strength to mourn in peace.

May I find the strength to mourn without shame or embarrassment.

May I find the strength to mourn out loud and cry until my crying is done.

May I find the strength to mourn with patience and be tolerant to move through this at my own pace.

May I find the strength to accept that I am in mourning and be at peace with that while my heart mends.

May mine be a good mourning, one that cleanses my heart and renews my inner being.

May my memories of my beloved _____ comfort me so that I may be ready to love again.

Through_____, we learned compassion.

Through_____, we learned patience.

Through_____, we experienced joy.

Through_____, we learned to think about someone other than ourselves and we learned both giving and forgiving.

Through_____, we learned about friendship and loyalty.

Through_____, we learned about innocence and humility.

Through_____, we were given the greatest gift of all, unconditional love.

Through this beloved animal, we were shown the best qualities of humankind and found that the highest virtue of all is kindness to others.

As we go forth from this day, may these important lessons be within our hearts. It is in sharing them with others that we truly honor the memory of_____ and keep his/her spirit in our lives.

In the rising of the sun and in its going down,
We will remember.
In the blowing of the wind and in the chill of winter,
We will remember.
In the opening of buds and in the rebirth of spring,
We will remember.
In the rustling of leaves and in the beauty of autumn,
We will remember.
When we are weary and in need of strength,
We will remember.
When we are lost and sick at heart,
We will remember.
When we have joys we yearn to share,
We will remember.
So long as we live, our companions, too, shall live
for they are ever a part of us.
We will remember.

If you feel your client may need more support than you can give, consider helping them find a reliable, effective pet loss support group. Over the years, I have met people that held onto their grief and sadness more than others, and without their circle of friends going through similar losses, they would have really struggled to regain balance in their life. Pet loss groups commonly meet weekly or monthly and range in size from 1-2 people up to larger groups of 10 or more. You can even establish your own.

It can be difficult to judge who will need extra support and who will not. Keep support group information on your website or in your brochure for them to access on their terms. You can reassess how they are doing during a follow-up call a few weeks after the pet's passing and remind them that groups are available if they need. If gathering with strangers is too hard for them, try to offer some of your own time and just listen for a while if you can. Being available to them through all aspects of their loss is very important and will build a strong bond between you. Remember, many human hospice groups continue support 13 months past the death of a loved one. What can you do to support your families?

Compassion Fatigue

Compassion fatigue is a relatively new term for an old concept. It is the mental and physical exhaustion that often accompanies end-of-life caregivers. The work we do lends itself to sadness and anyone performing euthanasias long enough will become worn out on some level.

For most of us, euthanasia work is VERY rewarding, but as with any kind of career, burnout does happen. It is important for veterinarians to take care of themselves emotionally when performing end-of-life care work. Taking vacations and/or engaging in healthy, and fun local activities will help hold off fatigue and keep everything in better balance.

If you are starting out on your own and find yourself working everyday including overnight emergencies, do your best to limit the number of appointments you see per day or try to schedule regular breaks. When I first began my service, I allowed families to pick their appointment times, which made it very hard for me to balance my time effectively. Now, I schedule appointments closer together in an effort to finish my day at a reasonable hour. Personally, I find it mentally exhausting to help more than five families per day. If I need to take an hour off and go to lunch with a friend, get a massage, or spend time with my kids, I do it to help me regroup and replenish my energy. It is also important to eat regularly and drink plenty of fluids when on the road. This will help you keep your focus and prevent both mental and physical fatigue.

It might be necessary to sign yourself up for some therapy classes to talk and vent about your frustrations or share your joys. Many euthanasia specialists also continue to do general private practice work to help them find balance. Seeking therapy is not an admission of weakness, but rather demonstrates your desire for personal growth. If traditional therapy is not for you, remember, you have colleagues all over the country experiencing similar the same ups and downs. The personal connections I have made keep me energized and moving forward even during hard times. On a personal note, should the time come when one of your own beloved pets needs help, consider having another vet perform the euthanasia. Focus your mental strength on supporting your pet and let someone else manage the technical part.

Death: What to Expect

I always tell my families that death is a very individual event, and it is impossible to completely predict how it will occur. When an animal dies, it goes through a series of system shutdowns. With the administration of a barbiturate, cerebral death occurs first, then the respiratory and cardiac centers of the brain shut down, and, if euthanasia is done properly, this occurs in such a way as to prevent suffering. We know that the body will go through certain changes that are universal to all animals. To what extent an individual exhibits these changes depends on the animal's health, the presence of a sedative, the method of euthanasia, etc. These physical signs include agonal breathing, myoclonus or muscle twitches, body stretches, defecation, and more. Some of these signs can be lessened based on your sedation protocol, route of pentobarbital administration, etc. Let's explore why these changes occur and ways we can explain them to a family to offer reassurance that they are perfectly normal.

Unconsciousness – Cerebral Death

Once cerebral death has occurred, the pet may still exhibit subtle or more obvious physical movements like leg stretching or muscle twitches. If a pet exhibits any of these signs, let the family know that their beloved pet is completely unaware of anything it is doing. It is sometimes difficult for them to see these motions and believe that their pet feels none of it. Remind them that there is  no pain anymore, and that the pet is peacefully embracing death. For our purposes, this state of unconsciousness is synonymous with cerebral death. A few studies have been done to test the time from barbiturate injection to cerebral death, and the findings indicate that cerebral death occurs almost simultaneously with the drug reaching the brain. Therefore, the pet is unaware of any post mortem side effects such as stretching, urinating, or agonal breathing.

Respiratory Arrest

The second stage of death is the cessation of breathing, which is controlled by the breathing centers within the medulla oblongata of the brainstem. When the euthanasia agent takes effect, you will sometimes see a change from rhythmic breathing to a short burst of rapid, shallow breaths, but a cessation of breathing altogether, also known as apnea, quickly follows. Once the breathing centers have stopped working, the pet may still exhibit agonal breaths. These are purely reflexive. Agonal respiration is a pattern of breathing sometimes seen around the time of death characterized by irregular inspirations usually separated by long pauses. The pet may also open its mouth widely, make a "gasping" sound, and curl its body with each breath.

Agonal breathing may persist for several minutes after cessation of the heartbeat, and to families, it can look like suffocation. As far as I know, there is no way to stop agonal breathing once it begins. It is very important to prepare them for these breaths and assure them that they are very normal. They can sound worse if the chin is tucked low to the chest. I have received many late night phone calls from frantic people who are watching their pet die naturally, and, when agonal breathing begins, they are convinced that the pet is suffocating. I gently explain that the pet is in the last stages of dying and the best thing they can do is be there to support them. As I noted in the Sedation chapter, some sedatives will help lessen this side effect. If you want to decrease the likelihood of agonal breathing, personal experience and reports from colleagues suggest you should administer Telazol® or propofol before euthanasia. Also, slow administration of your euthanasia solution should help.

Death and agonal breathing are so closely connected that other animals in the household often appear to instinctually understand what is happening. In-home euthanasia offers a unique opportunity for other family pets to be present during death and witness firsthand the changes that happen. Because agonal breaths are so obviously different from normal breaths, other pets in the room will often come over to their dying friend at this time. They might sniff around or seek comfort from their owner.

> *One of my most memorable euthanasias came early in my career when I went to help an old yellow lab. Her health had been failing for the past year; arthritis made it almost impossible for her to walk, and obesity was making it hard for her to breathe. Her owner and I gathered with her in the*

hallway where she was most comfortable. When she died and gave a few agonal breaths, her two lab housemates came in from the other room where they had been resting, stood over the top of her and howled... loudly, I might add. They picked up on the changes she was going through and understood that she had died. Her owner looked at me with amazement and asked if their reaction was normal. He had never seen them act this way before. "No," I said. "It is a very special reminder of the deep connection these animals have to one another." We both smiled and felt blessed to be a part of something so extraordinary.

Cardiac Arrest

Cardiac arrest is the final stage of death. The primary goal of euthanasia is to stop the heart quickly with an absence of pain. Barbiturates work on the cardiac centers in the medulla oblongata, not on the heart itself as other drugs do. Once apnea occurs, the heart ceases to beat because of hypoxia as well. In most instances, the heart will stop beating within 30 seconds of administration and you can pronounce the pet deceased. It is well known that cardiac electrical activity can occur for up to 28 minutes after euthanasia, even though no physical signs of life remain. It really depends on the overall health of your patient and how fast the euthanasia drug took effect. When you are listening to the heart after administering the euthanasia agent, you are safe in saying that a pet has died even if you hear faint fluttering within the chest. The normal heartbeats have stopped, and you are picking up on the effect of these final electrical impulses. If you still hear regular heartbeats 90 seconds after an intravenous or intracardiac injection, something is not right. Re-examine your injection site to make sure the entire dose went into the vein. If it did not, give another full dose via an appropriate route. Once complete cardiac death has occurred, the chest will be silent except possibly for some movement of gas within the lungs, trachea, and esophagus.

Postmortem Side Effects

Euthanasia solutions are approved by the FDA based on the speed with which cerebral and cardiac death occur, but no consideration is given for postmortem side effects. Although the Center for Veterinary Medicine within the FDA would prefer an animal exhibit "no adverse events" once death has occurred, such side effects are possible with any of the current euthanasia solutions on the market.

By definition, postmortem side effects occur after death, and the pet therefore is unaware of any changes that affect its body. Common things to see are a stretch of the legs, back, and neck, curling of the tail, urination or defecation, muscle fasciculation, small twitches of the feet and whiskers, pupil dilation, eyelid opening, erect ears, tail hair fluffing, and agonal breathing. Some of these things, like muscle twitches and urination/defecation, can  occur for several minutes or more following death. Much of what we may observe around the time of death is caused by a loss of parasympathetic blocking and a pronounced sympathetic cascade. If you will be leaving the pet with the family for home burial, make sure they understand that these "energy-releasing movements" may continue for some time.

In general, I think it's safe to say that cats tend to pass more quietly than dogs. For my service, it might hold true due to our presedation of cats with Telazol®, but even dogs that receive the same protocol sometimes show postmortem side effects. Cats rarely stretch their legs, take deep agonal breaths, or defecate. Their transition into death is very subtle with the most obvious change being apnea. Dogs tend to take deeper breaths, have leg stretches, and commonly defecate. Exotics with IP injections pass very quietly with only the occasional agonal breath.

Rigor (Latin-"stiff") mortis (Latin-"in death") occurs when muscle fibers lack the energy to release their fibers. Rigor mortis typically sets in within an hour or so, at least enough to feel a difference when moving the pet's body. If a pet has been seizuring before euthanasia, it may develop in as little as 10 minutes. Internal and external temperatures and the pet's overall health at the time of death also affect the time of onset. The pet's body will remain in this state until decomposition begins and the muscle fibers break down. I've seen this start in as few as 36 hours up to 72 hours after death. If the family will be keeping the pet for burial or performing a ceremony a day or two following death, make sure they know that the body will "soften" again. Also let them know about fly-strike and maggot infestation, which I will talk more about in the chapter on Aftercare.

In-Home Pet Euthanasia Techniques

We often assume that the faster cardiac death occurs the better. However, I would challenge that and say that equally as important when a family is present is a smooth transition to unconsciousness and a lack of side effects. The faster cardiac death occurs with barbiturates, the greater the risk of side effects, thus demonstrating that faster isn't always better. As veterinarians, we want the pet to die quickly, but death should occur in such a way as to protect the family from seeing potentially disturbing side effects. The average person cannot tell exactly when  the heart has stopped. What they focus on are the agonal breaths and other outward signs of what they perceive their pet to be experiencing. Pentobarbital is a drug that elicits a rapid cardiac death, but there are other drugs and combination of drugs currently being studied that may be better. Veterinarians should specifically request the development of a drug that leads to rapid cerebral and cardiac death AND eliminates all postmortem side effects, especially when presedation is not an option.

Characteristics of an ideal euthanasia drug would be:

- Low viscosity
- Low volume dosing (i.e., high concentration)
- High freezing point
- Stable at room temperature
- Distinguishing color
- Minimal to no pain at the injection site
- Rapid unconsciousness – within 10 seconds
- Rapid cardiac death – within 60 seconds
- No postmortem side effects
- Cost effective
- Suitable for food animal or wildlife use
- Non-controlled

"Old age means realizing you will never own all the dogs you wanted to."

~ Joe Gores

Chapter 5

Paw Prints and Other Keepsakes

Offering a keepsake to grieving families is a wonderful, tender way to show how much you care and honor the pet you have helped. Most people want a keepsake but won't have one arranged or prepared when it comes time to euthanize. You can exceed clients' expectations by making something for them, either during the appointment or after.

Paw Prints

Polymer clay paw prints are popular keepsakes these days, and many people will request them. They are appropriate for any type of animal you are helping, be it dogs, cats, or even exotics like birds or rabbits. My service offers them to every family and close to 90% want them. White or terra cotta are the most popular colors.

Clay can be purchased from local craft stores or you can buy it in bulk online. The clay is usually a polymer base and will come in normal or lightweight formulations. The normal weight is good for use in shadow boxes or left out on display. The lighter version is good for making hanging ornaments. If you do not want to assemble clay kits yourself, a company called World by the Tail, Inc. based out of Fort Collins, Colorado manufactures pre-made clay setups. Their clay is specially formulated to be softer and easier to knead than most artist's clay found in stores. See the appendix for their contact information.

If you choose to buy your clay in bulk and assemble your own kits, I recommend purchasing a small scale to measure out exact quantities of clay. Around 4.4 oz of normal weight polymer clay makes a nice print for an average size pet. You should use a little more clay if the dog is over 120 pounds or so. To bring clay with you to an appointment, place it in a small plastic bag and keep the clay flat so you can fit it in your doctor's bag. My bag can hold four to six clay kits easily. Most types of clay need to be baked so my service places a sticker with baking instructions right on the plastic bag. Once the print is made, we lay it flat on the bag so it can be handled before baking and the family can read the instructions above it.

Whatever clay type you use, you will need to shape the clay into a symmetrical flat patty, usually in the shape of a circle or heart before making the paw print. Make sure your hands are clean and dry before kneading the clay. Your hydrogen peroxide soaked gauze pads can be used to clean dirty hands. If the clay feels cold and hard, 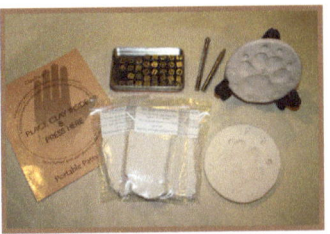 like it will if left in a cold vehicle overnight, hold it in your hands for a few minutes to warm it up. Cold clay does not make good impressions. Avoid forming air bubbles in the clay and smooth the edges free of cracks. Ideally, the patty will be at least one cm thick and large enough in diameter to hold the entire paw including nail impressions. Obviously for big dogs, your patty will need to be much larger than it would for an average sized cat.

When making a print, choose a paw that is clean, well shaped, and easy to manipulate. For example, the front left foot of a pet lying on its right side is a good choice because it is easy to hold, turn, and push into the clay. The back lower paw would be hard to angle correctly. People often worry about long nails, but they are easy to work with. The trick is to tuck the toes down to make room for them. If all of the paws are dirty, use the one that is cleanest and brush as much debris off as possible. If the paw is moist, try to dry it off a bit using your towel or a clean cloth. Do not try to wash off dirt with water. It will just make a bigger mess.

Some dogs and cats have a lot of hair between their pads. If they have been ill for some time or have been housed in an outdoor run, the hair might be very matted and even form what can look like another pad on a clay paw print. If necessary, trim some of the hair away with your clippers before making the impression. I personally like the look of a few whorls of hair. They add character to the print and make it unique to the pet.

To create the print, position the pet's paw in the middle of the clay patty, making sure to leave room for the nails and the pet's name. You will need to have something firm underneath the clay to push against, such as your binder or a clean hard floor. I use a small laminated card under the clay. Once you are positioned correctly, apply even pressure to the metacarpal/metatarsal pad first, and then follow with each individual toe. As you push you can roll the pad into the clay making sure to get every edge. Before you push down on each toe, try to "tuck" them down toward the metacarpal/metatarsal pad. This gives better detail to the phalangeal pad impressions and gives you room along the top for the nails. Be careful to keep the paw in the same position throughout to prevent distortion. If a pad has not made a good impression, just reposition it and push again. If your clay is cold or dry, you will have to push harder to make a deep impression. If the dewclaw has made a mark, you may leave it in or smooth it out.

Making an attractive print from a declawed cat's paw can be challenging. There is not much toe left to hold onto or press against. You can either use a back foot if those have not been declawed or do the best you can with a front foot. Most families seem to prefer a front foot regardless of how flawed it might look.

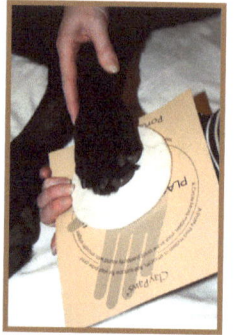

Now that the print is done, you can add the pet's name, years of life, etc. I like to put the name in the center along the bottom, but it can go just about anywhere. I use a stamping kit sold by World By the Tail, Inc. to make sure the letters are uniform and look nice. To center the name, start with the middle letter and work outward from there. You can personalize these prints with any of a number of embellishments, but be sure the family likes what you have chosen. Everyone is different. Remove as much debris as possible, and clean up little nicks and flaws. If you cannot remove all of the debris, it might be easier to brush away once the print has been baked. Let families know that they can add hair, trinkets, etc. prior to baking if they wish. Also, if they think they would like to hang the paw print, it is best to poke a hole with a straw at top of the clay patty before putting it in the oven.

If the clay does need to be baked, leave clear written instructions with the family. They will not remember verbal instructions in the midst of their grief. Some doctors like to take the clay home themselves to bake for the family and return it to them later on. Most clay will be fine if left unbaked for a few days or weeks, but it does remain soft and prone to damage so the sooner it is baked the better. When baking the clay, it is important to use a flat, glass-baking dish to prevent discoloration and burning of the clay. Below are my baking instructions for polymer clay:

Paw Print Instructions
Preheat oven to 275°F
Place clay on a flat glass-baking dish
Bake for 15-20 minutes
"Pop" loose with spatula. It will harden as it cools.

Keep in mind that clay may be seen as a tasty treat by other dogs in the house. Make sure the family keeps the unbaked print out of reach of other pets. I'll never forget the time I made a wonderful print and another dog in the house came right up and snatched it out of my hand. He tried to take it out into the yard, but we managed to stop him in time. Fortunately, the family thought it was quite funny so they baked the print with the other dog's teeth marks left in.

If you do not carry clay with you and the family wants a paw print, you can create a paper print using markers, an inkpad, or paint from the family's home. Clean the pads well and then color each individual pad, being careful not to color the surrounding hair. Once each pad is thickly coated, press the paw down squarely on a piece of paper. If the print is not dark enough, you can repeat the process or color in the print directly on the paper itself.

Years ago, I made an ink impression of a cat's paw for an owner. The print was not very dark so we just colored it in within the outlines of the print. The owner then took the paper to the local tattoo parlour and had her cat's paw print tattooed onto her back. Some families like ink nose prints and you can make these the same way as the paw prints.

Keepsakes from the Body

Over the years, I have had families request that we save various body parts for them, such as hair, toenails, eyelashes, whiskers, feathers, and even a skull. Even if a request seems strange to you, try your best to be accommodating. A family wouldn't ask unless it was important to them. Keep in mind that once the pet is buried or cremated, the opportunity will be lost.

Saving hair has been a tradition for centuries, and families may ask you to help them collect a nice sample during the appointment. I use my clippers because they allow for a very close cut that maintains the shape of the fur. As you can imagine, it is hard to obtain an intact collection of short hair with a pair of scissors. Have the owner prepare something to put the hair in so you can gently transfer it without losing the shape of the cut. You can take hair from anywhere the client wishes, but many like a sample from the neck where they have petted their friend for years. Eyelashes and whiskers are also easy to obtain by gently plucking. Just be very gentle and avoid damaging the skin. This is the case for feather collection too.

Toenail collection is a little more invasive than hair collection. When possible, wait as long as you can before cutting off a nail to minimize bleeding. Ten minutes following the death of the pet should be fine in most cases, but have your gauze out and ready just in case. To remove a nail, cut it off at its base with a pair of nail clippers.

Other body parts that are collected include reptile tails and scales, turtle shells, and rabbit tails. I even had one family request that their dog's skull be spared from cremation and preserved for display. At the last minute, they changed their minds, but we would have done it for them. Our local veterinary school agreed to prepare the skull for the owner for a minimal fee.

Other Keepsake Favorites

These days just about anything is possible in the realm of personalized keepsakes. You name it and it's probably available: portraits, jewelry, puzzles, and blankets made with a pet's picture, sweaters woven with pet hair, etc. If you want to exceed expectations, offer a variety of keepsakes from which families can choose. We sell some items on our website for later purchase, but we never try to sell merchandise during a euthanasia appointment.

As part of the mourning process, recommend that families do whatever they can to memorialize their pets. As I look back on the pets I have lost over the years, I treasure anything I have of them: collars, brushes, prints in the concrete, burial sites, and of course pictures. They put a smile on my face every time I come across them. The only way to move forward in healing is to reflect and remember. Keepsakes are a beautiful way to honor the soul.

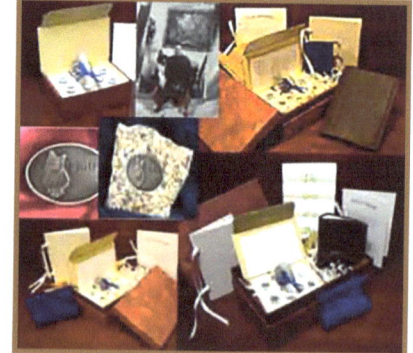

"We can judge the heart of a man by his treatment of animals"

~ Immanual Kant

Chapter 6

Transportation for Cremation

When it comes time to move your patient out of the home to your vehicle, using the utmost care and respect is very important. This will be the family's last memory of their pet, and it is your last chance to make a strong, impression on them. Presentation, timing, and safety are things to consider as you enter this next phase of the appointment.

Vehicle Arrangements

Your vehicle needs to have plenty of room to hold your patient. Pets should fit easily inside and lie in a natural position, not cramped in a seat. I strongly encourage you to use a vehicle that gives you the room you need. Many people will view your vehicle as a hearse, transporting their beloved pet on its final journey. A clean and comforting presentation will go a long way towards making the family feel that you care and are willing to go above and beyond. The area in your vehicle where you will be placing the body should be clean, free of trash and dirty towels, and no other deceased pets should be visible.

If your service is busy like mine, you may have to go from one appointment to the next without time to stop at the crematory. I keep room free in the back of my van where I can tuck the first pet under a blanket. If a family asks if another pet will be riding along with theirs, I am honest and say "yes, your sweetheart will be kept company by another friend" or something similar. Families are very understanding of this.

In an effort to keep everything clean and tidy, I keep a large plastic bin in the back of my van that holds a number of things that I use every day. In the "Making Preparations" chapter, I list what you might want to keep with you. Wet wipes are very important in this type of

service. They can keep your hands, shoes, the stretcher, your bag, and the interior of your vehicle clean. Be ready to clean up bodily excretions. I also keep a can of air freshener close by.

The bin is a good place to store nice blankets and towels for use during a euthanasia appointment and to tuck around the pet for the ride to the crematory. If towels get soiled, I tuck them away under clean ones and out of sight. I also keep large, durable plastic bags for use as body bags. They are not to be seen by families and do not get used until I am far away from the house or have arrived at the crematory. If you prefer, there are a few companies that make specialized body bags made of cloth or decorated plastics.

When you are ready to bring your patient out to your vehicle, leave the door open so you do not have to lay the animal on the ground or reach awkwardly while you open the car door. You have an opportunity to do this when you carry your things out to the vehicle and get the stretcher or wrapping blanket to bring back into the house. Most of the time your vehicle will be open and unattended for only a short period of time. If there are cats in the area, make sure none are inside your vehicle when you drive away. It happened to me once.

Moving the Body

Using a stretcher to move large patients is one of the best things you can do to avoid awkward moments at the end of the appointment. I prefer a rigid stretcher to a soft one. A rigid stretcher distributes the pet's weight evenly and prevents pocketing of the weight in the middle. Two people can usually lift any size dog using a rigid stretcher. I like to use one for any pet that weighs more than 30 pounds. The biggest dog I ever helped was a 250 pound Great Pyrenees mix, and two of us managed to hoist him up the 2.5 feet into the back of my van. A soft stretcher would not have supported him.

A rigid stretcher will also allow you to move a dog by yourself if necessary. The Jorvet stretcher I use has small wheels on one end and three straps evenly placed across it. You can secure the dog with the straps, lift the head-end up, and push it into the vehicle. The average person can easily move a 100-pound dog by themselves. When you get to your vehicle, place the end you are carrying in the back of your vehicle, brace the bottom end with your foot, reach down, lift the bottom end up, then slide it in.

When you lift a pet to place it on the stretcher, you want to support the body as evenly as possible. I usually ask a family member to use one hand to support the head and neck and the other hand to lift the lower front leg. I like to lift the hind end along with the towel to catch any urine or stool. Before you move the dog, make sure the person helping at the front has the head well supported. People do not realize just how different their dog's body will feel after death. Help them so the head doesn't drop or fall out of their hands. We will then slide the dog either forward or backward onto the stretcher. Moving a dog backward is easier because the legs do not get in the way. Once the dog is positioned centrally on the stretcher and the towel is tucked underneath the hind end for more protection, I check the mouth in case the tongue has slipped out. I then gently drape a nice clean blanket over the body up to the neck. I like to see the head and give the family opportunities for more contact with their pet, but this is personal preference. I often tuck a small, flat pillow under the head for an even softer presentation. Pets with airway disease, oral masses, and other conditions can release blood, serous fluid, or vomitus from their mouth and nose and the pillow helps soak these up.

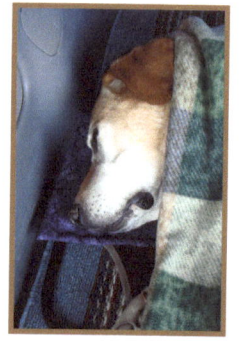

Once the pet is on the stretcher, family members can place special items around the pet like toys and bones for the journey. I tuck things under the upper front leg so it looks like the pet is cuddling them. I helped one family that completely covered their dog in special blankets, toys, and notes of love. All of it was cremated along with the dog. Most crematories are pretty accommodating as long as these extras are small. Sometimes it's nice to lift a dog using its bed and place it directly on the stretcher. The bed can be returned to the owner if they want, donated to a shelter, or it can be cremated with the pet if it's not too large. Big pet beds with a lot of stuffing create too much smoke during the cremation process, which clashes with EPA regulations.

If there are two people carrying the stretcher, one person will need to walk backwards through narrow hallways and doors. I like to do it because I am comfortable navigating this way and the other person helping can simply focus on the pet. If you can clear a path and open doors first, it will make this time easier for all involved. Make sure any doors you must pass through can accommodate the width of the stretcher, a dog's long legs, etc. Also keep other pets in the house safely out of your path.

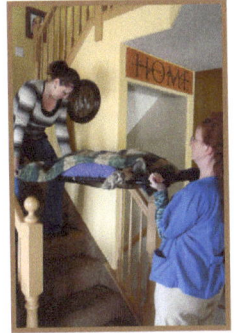

If you need to go up or down stairs, the stretcher and body should remain level. When going up stairs, the person walking backward will need to bend down very low and the person facing forward will have to lift the stretcher high, around chest level. When going down stairs, the situation will be reversed. If you have concerns about the strength of the person helping you, strap the dog securely on the stretcher first in case it gets dropped.

Once you reach your vehicle, guide your assistant on how to gently place the stretcher with pet inside. My van allows me enough space to place the stretcher parallel with the back of the vehicle. If your vehicle is not wide enough, you will have to place the stretcher in length-wise. When this is the case, keep the dog's head near the back of your vehicle so families can give some final kisses. If your pet will be lengthwise across the back, position them so their legs are facing toward the front of the vehicle. This way, if you have to slam on your brakes, the pet's legs will prevent it from rolling forward.

I recently met pet crematory owners from Canada. They shared with me that when practical, they transport pets to the crematory in caskets. They bring the casket into the home, gently place the pet inside and carry them out to the vehicle. After more discussion, I learned this is being done in the U.S. and other countries as well. If you are looking for that extra special touch to help your clients, this might be something you can do.

<u>Carrying the Body</u>

For smaller pets, a stretcher will not be necessary. When the family is ready to make the transition to the vehicle, wrap the pet in a large towel or appropriately sized blanket. Keep the towel you placed during euthanasia with them when lifting the body because moving the pet will often express the bladder or bowels. To lift the body, make sure the head, chest, and abdomen are all well supported. Remember that most of the weight will try to sink to the middle. The term "dead weight" definitely applies here. If a family member wants to carry the body, make sure they understand just how different their pet will feel. The head may droop, the legs will swing, and any compression of the chest may release air.

If the pet is small, cradle it like a baby, making sure the hind end is still tucked under the blanket. If the pet is too large to cradle, you can lift the pet with the legs facing downward. Support one arm behind the back legs and use the other arm to lift in front of the chest. The head will then rest on your arm or hang downward over it. The tongue may fall out in this position. You can almost always expect the bladder to express when carrying a large dog. If you can, keep the towel or blanket around its hind end. When you get to the vehicle, lay the pet gently inside, again making sure to support the head as best you can.

Final Moments

Whether you are using a stretcher or simply carrying the body, when you place the pet inside your vehicle, make sure your patient is still tucked in nicely and that he looks peaceful and well cared for. Now is the time for final goodbyes. Step back and allow the family to approach their pet for some parting words and love. Once they are ready, you can make sure they understand all the aftercare arrangements. I then initiate some form of closing gesture because this time can be so overwhelming that families don't know what to do. Many people like to give hugs and words of thanks. Be open to human contact and accept whatever the family wants to give, be it a handshake or a hug. Close the door to your vehicle slowly and with respect. You have very precious cargo. Pull away slowly and always assume you are being watched.

The special touches that you offer during this time will be remembered forever. Even if your client appears nonchalant, maintain your compassion and respectfulness. They will be grateful.

A dog facing outward is still acceptable, but the body may roll if the vehicle stops too fast.

"Dogs are not our whole life, but they make our lives whole."

~Roger Caras

Chapter 7

Aftercare: Cremation and Home Burial

Families have many aftercare options these days. A full service euthanasia doctor should offer assistance with aftercare to help keep things easy for the family. Depending on where you live, your clients will likely be choosing between cremation and burial. Your job is to educate families about their options and help them determine the best way to proceed given their finances, property type, and their overall wishes.

Cremation

Learn what your community has to offer with regards to cremation services. Do you have pet crematories nearby? Do they offer private and communal cremation? Will they come to a client's home or your office or do you need to bring pets to them? Make sure that any crematory that you work with has an excellent reputation. Take a tour of the facility and get to know the staff. If a family asks "How do I know it's my pet's ashes I'm getting back?" you want to be able to reassure them with the utmost confidence. If you have a strong relationship with your local crematory, they might allow you afterhours access so you can bring the pet there anytime. If this is not possible, consider having them come to you to pick up pets. Many euthanasia doctors have freezers at their offices for holding pets until the crematory can come. As pets become more revered as surrogate children, I encourage you to move away from freezer use and keep pets in "cooling rooms" until the crematory arrives.

Talk to the family about what is important to them. Private cremation is becoming more and more popular. Keeping a pet's ashes allows for a genuine physical connection to remain between pet and owner. Depending on the crematory, return of ashes may occur within 24 hours or take as long as a week or two. Make sure the client knows what to expect. Owners can choose to keep the ashes or spread them in a symbolic way. Many people plan to be buried with their pet's ashes down the line.

Some crematories offer semi-private cremations. This involves cremating multiple pets together and then giving a mixture of their ashes to each family. This option is usually more economical than a private cremation.

If keeping the ashes does not sound appealing, families can choose communal cremation. In these cases, their pet will be cremated with other pets and the ashes will be spread wherever the crematory designates. One of my local crematories spreads ashes throughout their pet cemetery grounds. Families can visit whenever they wish and enjoy a peaceful setting.

Whatever service the family chooses, make sure you identify the pet properly. Use an identification tag of some sort and fill out the necessary paperwork. Every crematory has its own system. Keep their supplies with you in your binder or vehicle so you can have everything ready by the time you arrive. Don't put yourself in a situation where there are questions about a pet's identity after cremation or a communal cremation was performed instead of a private one.

Collecting payment for both euthanasia and cremation during your appointment simplifies things for the family. Writing one check is easier, and the crematories like this knowing that whenever they refer to you, payment will be collected. Having payment out of the way also simplifies matters at the time of pickup or delivery of the ashes. We pay our local crematories twice monthly for all the cremations that we arrange.

If you live close to a veterinary school, you might be able to make arrangements for rendering with them. For lack of a better description, we call this a chemical cremation when talking to families. The body is completely broken down with enzymes so there is no ash remaining. It is a very economical form of disposal that appeals to some families. If the clients choose, they can donate the pet's body for teaching purposes prior to disposal so students and faculty can learn from their underlying medical condition.

<u>Burial</u>

Burial can be accomplished either on cemetery grounds or at the home. If your clients are choosing a pet cemetery burial, help them to make the necessary preparations. Contact the staff ahead of time to find out what they need done, such as the body tucked in a certain burial position or wrapped in a blanket. You should also learn the time of day euthanasia should be preformed when burial takes place on the same day. Find out how long it will take to prepare the ground and do they have a holding room for the pet before burial. Can they offer a funeral first? Cemetery burials are fairly expensive due to life-long grounds maintenance and therefore the family might prefer a home burial. On average, only 1 in 500 of our clients chooses cemetery burial. I'm sure that other parts of the country have a higher percentage than this.

Many families choosing in-home euthanasia want to perform a home burial. If you know this is what they want, you can provide them with a burial box or appropriate burial bag. A few companies out there make pet burial bags/containers, some of which are listed in the appendices. You can help prepare the body for them, including permanently closing the pet's eyes with a skin adhesive like Nexaband® or Vetbond®. A small amount along the edge of the eyelid is all you need to close the lids tight.

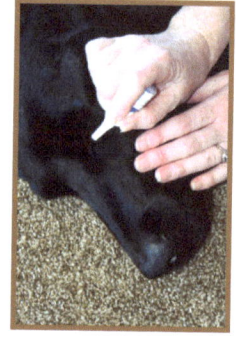

Being at home gives families the option of simply carrying their companion into the yard and laying them to rest without having to make the dreaded drive home from the vet's office. When possible, help the family move the pet to the burial site using your stretcher, the pet's bed, etc. Help them to lower the pet's body evenly into the grave. As nice as this can be for families, we need to educate them so burial is performed properly and legally. Across the U.S., many city governments have clearly stated laws prohibiting the burial of animals within city limits.

If burying is legal, proper guidelines should be followed. My county suggests these guidelines be used when burying a pet:

- Maintain a 100-foot separation from wells and waterways
- Maintain a 4-foot separation above the ground water table
- Bury the body with a minimum of 3 feet of soil cover
- Do not bury in a low-lying area, gully, or ditch that is prone to flooding

The best you can do is let families know about any local ordinances. Even if a family says they are going to take their pet to the local crematory themselves, there is nothing to really stop them from turning around and preparing a grave in their flower garden. If you know they are planning a home burial, make sure they understand how it should be done. Consider putting together a handout that will help them choose an appropriate location. Many people have never buried a pet before so there is a good chance they will do it incorrectly. Keep yourself legally protected by discussing these issues with your clients. You can even have them initial somewhere on your form to show that they understand their responsibilities. If you get the chance to see the burial site, do it. You can confirm that the preparations are appropriate.

Issues to touch upon include:

1. **Avoid buried utilities** – When preparing a burial site, families need to avoid buried water, gas, and power lines. I don't know of any veterinarians that have been held responsible for property damage, but I can see it happening if the family wasn't made fully aware of the risks.

2. **Proper Depth** – The ideal gravesite will be deep enough so that the pet can be covered with at least 3 feet of earth. I usually call it "earth" as it has a nicer sound than "dirt". This depth is important for two reasons: to keep the pet protected from the elements and predation and to keep the predators themselves safe. Most families do not think about the risk that the euthanasia solution in their pets' bodies poses to predators, but it is the concept of "predator death" that puts veterinarians at the greatest risk of legal problems. Quite a few years back, a veterinarian was prosecuted by his state for killing a bald eagle that had inadvertently ingested a euthanasia solution-contaminated carcass. This is also why wildlife biologists and field animal vets inject potassium chloride or even choose to shoot an animal instead of using a barbiturate. If the family is so inclined, there are composting methods to help speed the body's degradation.

3. **Avoid tree roots and rocky areas** – If you are able to help choose the burial site, point the family away from large trees. The roots will undoubtedly become an issue, and if they aren't careful, they will weaken or kill the tree. Digging a deep grave in rocky ground is also extremely difficult.

4. **Property ownership** – This may sound strange, but make sure a family buries the pet on their own property. Many people have thought it acceptable to find an open field somewhere and use it as a burial site. Make sure the family is either on their own land or has permission from another private property owner.

5. **Maggots** – I would be remiss if I didn't at least mention maggots at some point. Before you leave the family with a deceased pet, teach them about fly-strike and the risk of maggot infestation. We have all seen them at one time or another. I can usually sense them the moment I approach an affected pet. They have a distinctive smell and sound. What I hate about them is their indiscriminatory nature. They will infest both dead and living pets with skin lesions. Dogs will lie there and pant, try to lick the area, and/or cry out in pain. I have helped pets screaming in pain while their tissue is being eaten. If you find them on your patient, and the family has not, try to hide them if you can. There are few things more upsetting to a family than maggots.

I usually find them around the tail or in the groin region. These areas are warm, frequently moist due to incontinence, and hard for the pet to groom. If a pet has been bathed, and not thoroughly dried, any break in the skin barrier is fair game for maggots. Even the most pampered pet, living in a clean apartment, away from other animals, can get maggots. And the speed at which they set in is astounding.

The life cycle of maggots begins with the egg stage and ends in the larval stage of the fly. They are designed to eat quickly and that is exactly what they do. Since maggots are intermediary stages of the fly's life cycle, their life span as maggots is only around 8-10 days, after which they molt into the pupal stage and turn into flies. The entire maggot life cycle takes 10 days in a warm environment and up to a month in cold weather.

Maggot Life Cycle

Eggs

Common houseflies lay their eggs in rotting tissue by the hundreds. The eggs hatch in warm weather within the next 8-20 hours. The minute they hatch, the larave begin feeding on the material on which they were laid.

First-Instar Larvae

The hatched larvae appear creamy white in color and are 2-3 mm in length. The first-instar larvae feed on the surrounding food material and attain a size of 10 mm.

Second-Instar Larvae

Once the larvae attain the size of 10 mm, they enter the second larval stage. The larvae continue feeding and molt or shed their skin for the first time.

Third-Instar Larvae

As the larvae continue feeding, they grow to attain a length between 15 mm and 20 mm. These maggots range from a creamy color to a light brown or reddish color. They molt once again.

Maggots are voracious feeders and can feed continuously for 24 hours non-stop.

In-Home Pet Euthanasia Techniques

I thought I had seen it all until not too long ago, I was called out to help a family whose dog had died about 30 hours prior to my arrival. I was going to transport the body to the crematory for them. The dog was kept in a cool garage with a blanket laid over top. The husband pulled back the blanket to show me his beautiful friend only to find the worse case of maggot infestation I had ever seen. In less than 30 hours, the maggots had completely eaten the tail base down to bone. The family was devastated. No one expected it, including myself or I would have kept the dog covered. I did my best to comfort them, but what can you really say to make that memory go away. In an effort to protect them from any more trauma, I transitioned the dog by myself onto the stretcher, keeping his body covered the whole time. I promised them that he would be cleaned up when I arrived at the crematory. When I got there, I gently laid him out on the wash pad and pulled back the blanket. The skin had fallen off the back third of his body and the smell was indescribable. I washed him as best I could and then made special arrangements with the crematory to have him cremated immediately. He was a beloved dog, and I did not want him to undergo any more physical change like that.

When the family decides to keep a pet for burial, and maggots are already present, they can kill and clean them off first using the following products:

- Hot water
- Shampoo
- Hydrogen peroxide
- Alcohol- both pharmaceutical and liquor
- Hairspray
- Pledge®
- RAID® wasp, ant, or cockroach spray
- Draino®
- Any product with Permethrins

How the family chooses to prepare the burial site is up to them. They can use a shovel, a pickax, or a front-end loader. If you know of someone in your area that has digging equipment, see if they are willing to help families prepare burial sites. This will help ensure that it is done properly. When to prepare the site is also up to the family. In cold parts of the country, people may think to dig the grave before the ground freezes. If not, they may choose to keep their pet protected in a safe, cold location until the ground thaws. I know that cemeteries light controlled fires to thaw the ground to the appropriate depth, but this is not usually appropriate for families to pursue. In warmer regions, having the site prepared before euthanasia prevents the body from being exposed to the heat for too long. If the gravesite isn't ready, and you are feeling ambitious, you can certainly offer to help. I find it very cathartic to dig. And believe me, the family will never forget the fact that their vet was out there helping.

Disposal

I should at least mention that landfill disposal is still an option in most parts of the country. Before cremation services for pets became available, this used to be the only way to dispose of a pet's body other than burial. Most animal lovers do not consider this to be an appropriate way of handling a pet's body, but it is a personal decision and the family has the right to choose what they want. My service does not offer to bring deceased pets to the landfill.

"Never wear anything that panics the cat."

~ P.J. O'Rourke

Chapter 8

Potential Problems

<u>Aggressive Pets</u>

Working with animals can be very unpredictable. Most of the time, the variability in our work is what makes it pleasurable. The different cases we see and the people we meet keep the day interesting and rewarding. However, when our patient is hurting or scared, everything changes. Even the sweetest dogs or most docile cats can become aggressive when they are faced with pain, anxiety, and fear. By the time we, the euthanasia doctors, are called in, pets are usually afflicted with a terminal condition, be it heart failure, cancer, or debilitating arthritis, and they are suffering.

My preferred definition of suffering is "anything that denies us our true self." Physical or mental suffering can lead animals to do things they might not otherwise do, such as scratch and bite. To keep everyone safe, we must recognize this potential for aggression and be the voice of reason for owners who might not believe that their gentle pet could ever hurt anyone.

Sometimes euthanasia doctors also have to deal with animals that have a behavioral problem with no known underlying medical condition. Before proceeding with euthanasia, discuss the patterns or changes in behavior to determine if euthanasia is the only course of action. You may find that thorough, consistent behavior training could make a huge difference for the pet and the family.

Before you offer in-home euthanasia, you should have a basic understanding of the species with which you will work. Your veterinary education will be helpful, but hands-on experience is better. Do you know what a cat is saying when he puts his ears back? How about when a dog suddenly stops wagging his tail and stares into your eyes? What if your reptile patient holds open his mouth for an extended period of time? If you find yourself in an unexpected situation, pay attention to your instincts. They are an excellent guide as long as they are not ignored.

The AVMA euthanasia guidelines state that veterinarians should not euthanize a species he or she does not understand, in part so that unnecessary euthanasias do not take place, but also so that the people involved can handle the animals safely and with minimal stress. In short, familiarize yourself with the types of patients you will see. If you feel so inclined, keep restraint equipment such as muzzles, slip-leads, cat bags, and heavy gloves in your vehicle. Whatever the cause of the aggression, we will talk about how to handle these pets from a safety and restraint perspective.

Feline Restraint

The success of various methods of feline restraint depends almost entirely on the character of the cat in question. Some cats are born easy to handle and others are not. If you are dealing with the difficult type, the family usually knows it and will sympathize with you. They will understand if you need to firmly hold their friend to give the sedative as long as you show compassion throughout the procedure.

Hopefully the mere fact that you are in the home where the cat is more relaxed will make things easier than they would be in the clinic setting. Only when you start will you know for sure.

If an aggressive cat will let you approach him, move quickly. You may only get one chance to give the sedative before he becomes angry. Hold him by the scruff and stretch his body backwards along the arch of your forearm. This keeps his teeth and nails away from you. You can then inject your sedative into his thigh. As soon as you have injected, assess the cat's reaction. If he is comfortable, you can lessen your hold a bit and massage the cat's neck, being mindful that you may need to take hold again if his state of mind changes. Remember that most of the time, the family will be watching you and you don't want it to appear like you are causing their pet discomfort. There is nothing painful about this hold technique; it just looks unnatural. If the cat is angry after the sedative injection, maintain your hold and place a towel over the cat and your arm. The darkness and confinement can be soothing. As the sedative takes effect, you will feel the cat relax and you can then release your hold and allow the family to gather around. It will make them feel better to see their beloved pet resting peacefully before proceeding with euthanasia.

If the cat refuses to be held after the sedative injection, you can release it and let it go hide somewhere in the room. Once he is sleeping, you can take him out of his hiding place and proceed with euthanasia. When dealing with a cat that may try to escape, make sure you close up the room and eliminate escape routes before starting.

> *I'll never forget the time that I gave a cat sedation and as soon as I finished, he tried to get away. Instead of letting him go and worrying about finding him later, I held on while his nails gouged a beautiful wooden dining room table. Upon seeing this, I did let him go, but it was too late. The damage was done. He had managed to push the towel out from underneath him and exposed the wood.*

If the family knows that catching the cat will be difficult, have them put him in a small room, preferably a bathroom, closet, or small bedroom before you arrive. When you are ready, you may be able to simply throw a towel over the top of the cat and hold him down by applying pressure over the back of the neck. Once you have a good hold, you can lift up the towel and give the sedative. If necessary, you can also inject right through the towel. Just make sure the sedative makes it into the cat. If the towel method doesn't work, herd the cat into the smallest space possible like a laundry basket or trashcan and try again. Every home and situation is different. Be resourceful and creative, and above all, keep yourself and any other people present safe.

If all else fails and you cannot catch the cat, let the cat catch you. Cover your upper body in tough material like a leather jacket and thick work gloves. Borrow something from the family if you need to. When your body is protected, move your arm right up to the cat and let him grab on. Take hold of the cat anyway you can, and if he is under something, pull him part of the way out. Either give the injection yourself or have someone else do it. I do not let go of these cats until they are obviously sedated. If you know you are dealing with an extremely aggressive cat, I would try this method first. It saves a lot of time and energy for everyone.

One last word on aggressive cats. When euthanasia is scheduled, you can make arrangements with the family for them to give an oral sedative like acepromazine in the cat's food about two hours before the appointment. I suggest prescribing more than you normally would since the ultimate goal is euthanasia and you are dealing with a volatile feline personality. Many vets like to start out with aggressive cats by giving a squirt of a liquid sedative like ketamine or dexmedetomidine directly into the mouth. While you can successfully relax a cat this way, I personally have not found it necessary to do. Dry Telazol® powder combined in moist cat food can also work. The dosage I have found is 20mg/kg, but I have never used this myself. My experience is that oral presedation rarely works perfectly by itself.

Canine Restraint

A painful or fearful dog should be handled delicately and with great patience. They don't want to bite, but are easily pushed over the edge and will respond aggressively if they feel they have no other choice. In fact, some dogs will become aggressive simply because of the tension in the room (i.e., the family's sadness and worry). Your confidence and control over this type of situation is good for both the family and the dog.

When your canine patient prefers his space, give him as much as you can. Avoid contact with the dog until the very moment that you have to give the sedative. I focus on the family, the paperwork, and only acknowledge the dog when speaking kind words about how things will proceed. Then the family and I discuss the best way to approach the dog. For a mildly aggressive dog that still has an appetite, distracting him with a bowlful of treats may be all that is necessary to allow me to quickly give the sedative between the shoulder blades. If the dog still notices my movements, I have the owner position themselves between the dog and me. I realize this sounds dangerous, but it works very well. The dog feels much more secure and the owner can offer love and more treats. If we need to take a few extra minutes to make sure things go smoothly, we will. Once I give the sedative, I move away from the dog and wait while sedation occurs.

If the dog is very aggressive, I recommend you use a muzzle to protect everyone involved. Owners usually have the best luck with this so I will let them try first as long as they can do so safely. I show them exactly how to slip the muzzle on and emphasize that they cannot tighten the strap too hard. Once the muzzle is placed, give the sedative quickly and step back again. Have the owner remove the muzzle if the dog will allow it or keep it on until full sedation has occurred. I almost never euthanize a dog wearing a muzzle. It looks cold and untrusting during the dog's final moments.

There will be times when a dog cannot be muzzled. For these cases, you will need to restrain the dog in another way. If the dog can be leashed, either you or the owner should run the free end through something very secure, like through a fence post, a stairwell banister, or between a door and its jamb. Pull the leash so that the dog's head and neck are held tightly against the structure, and you can give the sedative quickly into the hind end. I always give intramuscular injections to aggressive dogs so that the drugs work a little faster. Of course, make sure the dog's collar is tight enough so that he can't slip out. You can also use a slip leash.

When you arrive, if a dog is recumbent but still aggressive, I recommend placing a large blanket over him and quickly applying pressure around the edges of the blanket near his head and upper body to prevent him from pushing his way out. Once you feel you have the dog secured, you can inject the sedative through the blanket or lift one side to access the body.

If needed, you can also give dogs oral sedatives ahead of the euthanasia appointment. Our standard protocol is to have the owners give five times the normal oral dose of acepromazine two hours before we arrive. Dogs seem to handle even these high doses very well. In fact, most aggressive dogs that receive five times the normal dose are only groggy when we arrive. They are still able to walk around, and their blood pressures remain strong. Even if we've given acepromazine ahead of time, we almost always still have to use another form of restraint to give more sedation via injection. Oral Telazol® at 20mg/kg can also be used for really aggressive dogs. Fortunately, the need for oral pre-sedation is rare.

Exotic Restraint

If your service will be offering euthanasia for exotic pets, I recommend familiarizing yourself with the husbandry of all the species you plan on helping. Read up on how to restrain birds, reptiles, etc. In my experience, most small exotics can be easily restrained using a towel. By the time the decision to euthanize has been made, they are usually too sick and weak to offer much resistance. Pocket pets like rabbits, ferrets, and rodents are also usually very debilitated by the time I arrive and are rarely aggressive.

Personal Safety

By definition, a housecall practice will have you the doctor, entering the home of people you don't know very well. As any police officer will tell you, this has an element of danger. It is up to you to assess the situation before you enter the home and find ways to minimize risk to your personal safety.

Your first line of defense against a personal attack is your instinct. You were born with it – USE IT. If you feel that something is not right, even on the phone, act on it. Bring another person with you to the appointment and inform your client that you will be doing so. If the person calling you is honest and good-hearted, he or she will never question your need to feel safe. And you can always refuse to take the appointment over the phone or once you've arrived if you feel threatened. Make sure someone close to you knows where you are going.

Your second line of defense is knowledge of your surroundings. Look around you when you enter the home. Where are the exits? Are there neighbors close by? Do you know who is in the house? How will you get out and where will you go? I always keep my car keys in my clinic jacket in case I need to make a quick exit.

Your third line of defense is a defensive weapon of some sort and the ability to ward off an attacker. I carry pepper spray in my bag. Whatever you choose, keep it close at hand and know how to use it. I also recommend taking a physical defense class. These classes teach what to look for in an attacker, how to keep yourself out of dangerous situations, and how to defend yourself if the need arises.

There are other dangers to consider besides physical harm brought on by another person. I often find myself in very strange places when euthanizing pets, such as under decks or trees, in the back of trucks, along riverbanks, etc. Be careful not to hurt yourself. If you need to, you can always sedate a pet wherever they are, and once they are sleeping, move them to a safer place for you and the family. Try to keep the area well lit so you can see where you are going. Carry a flashlight in your bag. The family of the pet you are helping does not want you to get hurt either. Ask for help when you need it to ensure that things run smoothly. I once sprained my ankle on a missed step because I didn't want to bother the family and ask where to find the switch for the porch light. I was able to hide my injury until I was gone but then drove home in tears. Lesson learned!

"You think dogs will not be in heaven? I tell you, they will be there long before any of us."

~ Robert Louis Stevenson

Chapter 9

Common Questions from Clients

For most people, euthanasia is a very scary thing. They don't know what to expect and therefore will have many questions. Most of these questions can be answered over the phone during the initial call. Some families will be prepared with a list of things to ask you. This helps to put their minds at ease and makes your job easier during the appointment itself.

Following is a list of common questions I get asked by my clients. It will hopefully prepare you to answer similar questions and give some insight into what people are thinking about as they struggle with the decision to euthanize. Even though I could write volumes here, the answers will be short and concise. I have written the answers as if I was talking directly to the client.

1. Is euthanasia painful?

If done properly, no. When the euthanasia drug is given directly into the vein, the pet should not feel anything. Any bodily movements the pet undergoes once the drug is given are purely involuntary, like a reflex. With barbiturate overdoses, the brain loses consciousness, followed quickly by respiratory and cardiac arrest. If another method of euthanasia is performed, such as an intracardiac injection, anesthesia will be given to eliminate pain. After all, euthanasia means "good death" and pain is not appropriate.

2. How will I know it's the right time to euthanize?

You know your pet better than anyone. Watch for signs that tell you she is not happy anymore. I encourage you to make a list of three things that she likes to do. If she stops one of them, you are getting close. If she stops two, you need to do something, either dramatically increasing her treatment protocol or talk with your family about letting her go. The list can become the pet's voice when your emotions cloud your judgment. We get so used to a pet's new diseased condition that we forget what she used to be like, what she used to enjoy. We accept this new "normal" and pray she doesn't worsen even more.

Every week I hear people say things like "She hasn't been able to stand for three days, she stopped eating about five days ago, and she doesn't want to be touched. She has been declining and losing weight for about six months, but today she wagged her tail. Am I being hasty about this?" My reply is that only you know for sure, but I consider this a good moment in an otherwise bad day. Look for the time when the bad days outweigh the good. There is no rule or law that you have to choose euthanasia. We choose it because we want to end suffering.

After euthanasia, many people say to me that they waited too long. No one has ever said that they made the decision too early. It is our overwhelming love and devotion to our pets that makes letting them go so hard. Talk to your family; open up the communication now so that you are ready for whatever happens.

3. I don't want my pet to suffer. Does he need to be close to a natural death before you will euthanize?

If we know he has a terminal condition, and you are not going to pursue treatment, then I am willing to help you whenever you need. I would rather help your pet pass sooner than before unquestionable suffering has set in. In fact, there is a saying pertaining to euthanasia that goes "I would rather help my friend a month too early than an hour too late." It is impossible to know when that "hour too late" will be until it has already arrived so if you are choosing to be proactive, I support you. The only time euthanasia becomes an easy decision is when your pet is so miserable that you cannot help him fast enough. If you want to prevent suffering, I'm here for you. I would love to help your pet on a good day, when he is still open to affection, breathing comfortably, and not consumed by his disease. If you feel helping your friend reach a natural death is more fitting for your family, and euthanasia is too much to consider, we should talk about hospice care.

4. Is there anything I can do to make him more comfortable as his condition progresses?

Absolutely. This is the time for hospice care. We need to get him started on appropriate medicines or supplements to manage pain, infection, and help slow the progression of the disease. We also need to maintain good hydration, with fluid therapy if necessary. Dehydration is very uncomfortable and leads to poor body heat regulation, digestive problems, immune system weakening, and general malaise. If your pet is unable to walk, you need to help him up so he can urinate and defecate away from his bed. You also need to turn him from side to side so he doesn't get pressure sores. Providing proper nutrition is very important too. Your pet needs to eat appropriate, easy to digest foods to provide him with energy and the dietary building blocks necessary to maintain the body. Your vet can help you with this, or I can get you started too.

If you are open to outside help, I recommend physical therapy, acupuncture, chiropractic adjustments, massages, and if possible, some old fashioned mental stimulation. Get out his toys, take him on car rides, have play dates, etc. Whatever your pet might like is great. As we know, at the end it becomes more about the quality of life than the quantity.

5. Does she know that she's about to die and will she be scared?

To her, my presence does not mean she's going to die. When I enter your home, I'm just a friend who has come to visit. I present myself very gently and with good intentions. If she is nervous and shakes at the vet's office, it is safe to say that she is afraid, and this is what we are trying to avoid by providing in-home euthanasia. The whole idea is to provide a peaceful, gentle death, one free of stress and worry.

Many of my patients like to snuggle next to me while I discuss things with the family. And giving sedation just helps to ensure that even if your family's anxiety level increases, she will remain calm and relaxed. Many pets are made nervous by the stress they feel from their owners.

6. I'm worried about my dog's blood pressure. Are you going to be able to find a vein?

Euthanasia can only be accomplished by getting the solution into the blood stream. As with any medical procedure, things can be straightforward or more complicated depending on the physical health of the pet. In-home euthanasia is unique because you will be present for the technical parts of euthanasia, such as catheter placement. If we were in the clinic, she might be taken into the treatment area, away from you, and the catheter placed in privacy. When ill pets go into the clinic, their anxiety will raise blood pressures making catheter placement relatively easier than in the home. The beauty of being at home is a relaxed pet and therefore sometimes weaker pressures. If her veins have been good in the past, we should be just fine. That being said, there are times, albeit rare, when veins are impossible to find. I will try to locate one on the leg that is the easiest to use, and if her veins are not cooperating, I will continue to other legs and try until one is found. If it proves impossible, we can move to another method of euthanasia such as an intracardiac injection. This time can be challenging for the family, but she will sleep through everything. I always start with the intravenous method because it is what most families expect and is, physically speaking, the easiest to bear witness too. Some families have a very hard time watching a cardiac injection or something similar. I will do my best to keep the time with her pleasant and comfortable for all present, even if her catheter placement is technically challenging.

7. Should my other dogs/cats be present for the euthanasia of their housemate?

Many families chose in-home euthanasia specifically to allow other pets to be present. My personal thought is that you should allow them to be there if they want, but I don't like to force anyone to be present if they are uncomfortable. The unique thing about other animals is that you cannot simply tell them their friend is dead. They really need to discover it for themselves, and being present during the death is the best way. I have never experienced or heard of any detrimental effects when a dog or cat witnesses death. If you choose for them to be absent, I recommend you give them a chance to see the body afterwards. Many times they do not demonstrate an obvious understanding about what has happened, but at least they have had the opportunity.

8. Should I allow my kids to be there?

I personally feel that kids do wonderfully when allowed to be present. They ask questions, they see how peaceful it can be, and they learn how to grieve openly for their friend. Some kids really open up and cry, even sob, which I think is very healthy and important. A lot of children have grown up with the pet in question and want to be there to say goodbye. They may have never known life without them.

When I was 10 years old, our Great Dane was hit by a car and broke her back. My dad took her to the emergency clinic where they euthanized her. To this day, I wonder what her final moments were like. Was she scared?

Did things go easy for her? Kids tend to have over active imaginations and having them present can help keep things balanced.

If you choose to keep the kids away, there are some good ways to help them into the mourning process. I have seen some families release balloons into the sky as a way of symbolizing the release of the spirit. Some families put together scrapbooks, make up songs about their friend, draw pictures, etc. If you are keeping the ashes following cremation and plan to bury them, you can have a ceremony with the whole family.

The important thing with children is to allow them to grieve, and acknowledge that this may be harder on them than you might realize. The loss of a pet is often their first experience with death and it is up to your family to make it a healthy experience. Be honest with them regarding what is happening and avoid confusing phrases like "going to sleep." Many children have lost sleep over this misguided phrase.

9. My dog hates new people, especially vets. Are you going to be able to give him the sedative?

We'll be just fine. With your help, we can give him lots of love and get him to focus on you rather than me. If he still loves treats, he can have as many as he wants while I quickly give him the sedative. It's just like giving a vaccine, and most dogs don't even notice it. If we feel it's necessary, we can always muzzle him for the sedative injection and then take it off so he can relax while it takes effect. Most of the time, this goes much easier than people expect. Remember, I don't look like a vet in your home. I'm just a friend who has come to visit.

10. What if I can't watch? Do I have to be there?

You do whatever feels right. Since we're at your home, you can step away at anytime. I will proceed with things, and you can come back in after your pet has passed or you can stay in another room. You can even leave the house if you need. If you want to be with your pet as he falls asleep, you can stay for sedation and then leave once he is no longer aware of his surroundings. I can take care of everything by myself if that is easier for you.

11. Will my dog urinate and defecate?

Not necessarily. This is very individual. If they do, I will have already tucked my towel underneath them for protection. I don't want you to worry about this. We can gather together anywhere you want, and I'll take care of protecting your home.

12. Why do the eyes stay open?

The simple answer is that your pet will not have the desire to close them. Death stops everything. Your pet might actually open his eyes a little upon death. This is very natural. If it makes you more comfortable, I can permanently close the eyes with a little skin adhesive applied along the edges of the eyelids. This is a common request for pets staying at home for burial.

13. How long will everything take?

We are usually with families anywhere from 45 minutes to an hour. If you want us in and out quickly, we can be done in as little as 20 minutes or so. We always allow for an hour with you and if you need more time, we'll make arrangements to be there as long as you need. You just let us know what you need and we can schedule our time accordingly.

14. How do you really know he's dead?

Listening to the heart is the best way, but there are many other signs that tell me death has come. I look for subtle body movements, reflexive breathing, and a glazing of the eyes. The eyes truly are the windows to the soul. They change immediately with death. You are always welcome to listen for a heartbeat with my stethoscope too. Sometimes hearing the quiet for yourself brings peace of mind.

15. Should I get the paw print?

If you are not sure, I would do it. You don't have to keep it, but if you don't have one made and you decide later you want it, the opportunity will be gone. They really are quite nice and something I think you'll treasure for years to come. Keepsakes may not seem necessary initially, but as time moves on, they can really warm the heart. I had one client get upset with me because I did not force him to do the paw print. During our appointment, he said he didn't want it so I moved on. A week or so later, he regretted that decision and told me I should have made him get it.

In-Home Pet Euthanasia Techniques

16. Can I witness the cremation?

You will have to ask the crematory to see if they can accommodate you. Some crematories welcome owner-present cremations, but others simply do not have the capability because of the way their facility is designed. If you are present, please know that even though the crematory staff will be kind and gentle, cremation itself is not necessarily a pretty process. They are burning the body and that is exactly what you will see. Some bodies ignite even before the door is closed. Just be prepared and make sure this is what you want to remember. If you just need to be sure of your pet's identity, you can witness them preparing your pet's body before cremation and be there as they collect the ashes after.

17. What do the ashes look like?

When cremation is complete, white bone fragments remain. These will be ground down into small bone fragments that look like tiny pieces of gravel. When you receive your pet's ashes, they will look like a gray powder mixed with these small white pieces.  Most crematories put the ashes in a clear plastic bag and place the bag within an urn or keepsake box.

18. Do I have to bury my pet right away or can I wait a few hours?

I think you should spend all the time you want with your friend. There is no reason to rush a burial if you need time to mourn over the body. Make sure your family and friends understand that this time is important to you and do what you need.

Yes, your companion's body will start to change. Rigor mortis can set in fairly quickly depending on a pet's condition at the time of death, but this is natural. If you have your burial site prepared, and the dimensions of the grave or burial box is set, I recommend tucking your pet's body into a position that will fit the available space. It is not easy to bend the legs or tuck the head once rigor mortis develops. Some families keep their pets above ground for many days, and the body actually softens again after 24-36 hours.

19. Who do we need to tell about her passing?

I would tell anyone involved in her life (e.g., her groomers, her daycare, etc.) I will notify her vets for you and whomever else you want me to.

Kathleen Cooney, D.V.M.

If you are concerned that her condition is hereditary, you might want to call her breeder. They should know about her health so they can make appropriate breeding decisions. And make sure to tell the people in your life like friends, family, and employers. If you have children, you might want to inform their teachers. You may need some time and space to mourn, even if it's only for a day or two. Hopefully everyone will understand.

20. Why won't he just die in his sleep?

Most owners hope for this. What a blessing for everyone if he would just quietly pass in night, and we wake up in the morning to find him gone. We know that if we do nothing, eventually he will. Nature will take its course, and eventually he will die on his own. The problem is that there is no guarantee that it will be peaceful and pain free for him. The way I look at it, he's been weakening every day and if you have been hoping that he will just pass in his sleep, the time has come to consider euthanasia. If you cannot make this decision, we need to talk about making him as comfortable as we can until a natural death occurs.

21. Are you a veterinarian?

Yes. You have to be a veterinarian to perform euthanasia in the home like this. Being a vet is important so that I can help guide you in your decision-making and help your pet pass peacefully using the appropriate drugs and equipment.

22. How much is all this going to cost?

My fees are based on travel distances, supplies, time, aftercare arrangements, and whether or not the appointment takes place during normal business hours. Some people think that all I do is give a shot, and the fee for the service shouldn't cost anymore than the drug I give. What I also do is calm the pet and family, provide sedation to relieve pain and anxiety, euthanize with expert technique, offer the paw print keepsake, prepare the body, and provide for transportation to the crematory. Clients also have unlimited time on the phone with me for consultation and help with the decision making process. You have enough to deal with during this difficult time. Let me make the experience as stress-free as possible and bring you some peace of mind.

23. What happens if someone asks you to euthanize a pet and you don't think it's time?

The best thing I can do is listen to the full story and try to determine what is best for everyone involved. People request euthanasia for their pets for so many different reasons. As a veterinarian, I need to make sure that the pet's best interests are taken into account. If a pet has a terminal condition that the family does not want to treat, I will euthanize rather than let the pet suffer through a long difficult death. If an aggressive cat is attacking and injuring its elderly owner and no one is willing to adopt it, I will euthanize rather than have them bring it to the humane society where the cat will be scared before being euthanized anyway. On the other hand, a blatant case of convenience euthanasia, like a young healthy dog that won't stay in the yard is another matter entirely. Long story short, I try to be open-minded and non-judgmental, and things tend to work out as they should. My newly adopted Chihuahua is living proof that I don't euthanize just because someone asks me to.

24. Does euthanizing pets wear you down?

Yes and no. It's a very challenging line of work, but very rewarding at the same time. If you'd have asked me fresh out of vet school if I wanted to be a euthanasia specialist, the answer would have been "no." Now after nearly 4 years, I cannot imagine doing anything else. Those of us who provide euthanasia are familiar with the notion of compassion fatigue. I think it hits some harder than others. I like to focus on the positive during appointments, like the relief of suffering for the pet and the peace I can provide for all involved. The pets I get to work with and the people I get to know keep me going even on the hard days. If anything wears me down, it's being on call for emergencies. I might help six families during the day and then get called out in the middle of the night. It's hard to get caught up on rest and recharge my batteries.

25. This is such a wonderful service. Are there more vets like you out there?

Yes. There are more and more euthanasia specialists starting their services every month. As more people request help for pets in their home, veterinarians will need to specialize and be ready when the need arises. Over the years, I have received hundreds of calls from people across the country who had found our website, but couldn't find anyone locally to help them. My company created a national in-home pet euthanasia directory listing veterinarians willing to make euthanasia house calls for non-regular clients. We work hard to grow the directory membership and find compassionate doctors who believe in saying goodbye in the comfort of home. If you know of a friend or family member who needs help with pet euthanasia or end-of-life care in their area, have them go to www.inhomepeteuthanasia.com.

"Blessed is he who has found his work: let him ask no other blessedness."

~ Thomas Carlyle

Chapter 10

Starting a Euthanasia Service

Before getting started in a service dedicated to end-of-life work, you need to do a little soul searching. As rewarding as I find it, others view it as depressing and emotionally draining. This field in veterinary medicine puts you into some stressful situations, both mentally and physically, and it demands that you always be ready to support families and pets. Are you ready to devote countless hours to phone time? Are you ready to drop everything you are doing to head out on an emergency call? Is your family prepared to help you start your own business, with all the associated ups and downs?

This is the time to talk to other veterinarians immersed in this line of work. Ask them how their business is growing, how they got started, what the pet-loving demographics in their area are, and how they are managing their work and home life. If the time is right for you to make the leap into end-of-life care, you can learn from my progression towards opening my own company. Here are the steps that I took listed in the approximate order of occurrence.

- Contacted local emergency vet hospitals and pet crematories to see the number of in-home euthanasia requests per day.
- Contacted local mobile vets to see if there was a need for a euthanasia specialist.
- Chose a good, uplifting company name.
- Wrote a business plan to identify the species I would be working with, my hours, my travel range, and philosophies.
- Purchased an appropriate vehicle for work and family (paid for through personal account).
- Spoke with an accountant to determine the appropriate business entity (e.g., LLC or Corporation) and discussed my plans with an attorney.
- Obtained a PO Box for my business mailing address (later I did not need it).

- Filed for federal, state, and city tax identification and licensing.
- Created payroll and sales tax accounts with city and state.
- Set up an office space in my home for record keeping, paper work, etc.
- Opened a business bank account with checks and debit card.
- Updated my controlled drug information and reviewed regulations.
- Updated my professional liability coverage to include mobile vet work.
- Opened workers compensation and unemployment insurance accounts.
- Took my major competition out to lunch to find ways to partner and grow simultaneously.
- Opened an account with my veterinary equipment and drug supplier.
- Hired a logo, website, and brochure designer.
- Opened up accounts with various suppliers: clay paw print kits, sympathy cards, pet loss books, printers, etc.
- Ordered enough drugs and supplies for at least 20 appointments.
- Began a few business management classes at the local small business development center.
- Bought a wall safe to hold controlled drugs and acquired a drug-log book from AAHA.
- Ordered QuickBooks® and learned how to use it.
- Opened a credit card processing merchant account to handle credit card payments.
- Designed my consent form and other handouts for clients and had a lawyer review them.
- Approved my logo, website, and brochure design after a few revisions.
- Drafted up a letter of business intent to send to local veterinary practices.

- Chose a uniform-type smock coat and had my logo stitched on it (it still represents our doctors to this day).
- Ordered 500 brochures and magnets and 1000 business cards to send to local vet practices to introduce myself and the unique service I was bringing to the area.
- Met with the local pet crematories to learn about their staff, policies, and facilities.
- Joined a business leads group and my local Veterinary Medical Association to network.
- Purchased some ad space in local newspapers and placed a small listing in the phonebooks.
- Offered to provide a lunch information session about my service for veterinary staff at local clinics (no takers at the beginning).
- Was granted after-hours access to all local crematories and made arrangements for pick-ups at my home (had a freezer provided by a crematory).
- Bought a comprehensive road map and nice towels and blankets for appointments.
- Had my first appointment call!! (Came in two weeks after my first brochures went out)

Total time = 2.5 Months   **Total cost = $4500**

I'm sure I have left some minor things out, but overall this is a good representation of the early days of my service. The total cost reflects all of my supplies and business startup costs. You can see that in comparison to opening a traditional veterinary clinic or even a more comprehensive mobile practice, the start up costs are very low.

As with any small business, you will have high points and low points. I finished my first year averaging 10 euthanasias a week. By the end of the second year, I was up to 20. Today, my service helps over 70 families per week.

Low points come when your appointment numbers plummet for no apparent reason. I once found myself helping 20 families a week for 5 weeks, 11 families per week for 2 weeks, and then I jumped to 30 families the next week. The work always seems to balance out, but it might take a few months and the variability can be stressful. I also find that pet death and associated diseases flow together in patterns. Our doctors will help six Golden Retrievers with lymphoma in one week and then no more for a month. We can help five cats with renal failure in one day. One of the most memorable patterns for me was the week we helped eight boxers with various conditions. These sweethearts accounted for one-third of our patients that week. There are patterns in the weather too. It is very rare for me to be out on a rainy or snowy day. Our families tend to call on milder days unless there is an emergency. As far as middle of the night emergency calls go, I might be called out three times in one week and then not again for six weeks. Holiday seasons tend to be busy too.

The trick to balancing out your appointment numbers is to keep marketing appropriately throughout the year. Hire a marketing team to help keep you focused on your goals, and bounce your ideas off them. Their job is to make you money without you having to work harder. "Make more in less time" as my marketing woman says.

When a slow time of year is coming up, we put out an informative newsletter to the clinics to remind them of what we offer the community. We donate items for charitable silent auctions. You might try to get an article about your work in the local paper or participate in a local pet expo. Everything you do helps you grow your client base, but of course some things work better than others. Even ads in newspapers and magazines will increase your business. I have started offering CE lectures to local clinics on euthanasia and hospice care, which allows them to become more familiar with my work and subsequently feel comfortable referring to me. For the general public in your community, you can become a resource on end-of-life care and pet loss support through a regular lecture series.

When my appointment numbers reached 20 per week, I hired an accountant to handle my book keeping and shortly thereafter, I took on a receptionist to help with scheduling and basic clerical work. When I really started examining my time commitment to each appointment, it came in at around 2-3 hours spent on each family, depending on travel time. The initial phone consultation, drive time, actual appointment, follow-up paper work, supply ordering, etc. were all factored in. Twenty appointments per week meant I was working more than a full time job, and it became necessary to hire help. Looking back, I wish I would have brought on help sooner to prevent those long evenings of paperwork trying to catch up after appointments were done. It was around this time that I also hired on veterinary associates.

If you find yourself needing help managing your appointment workload, find another doctor who shares your philosophies, has strong technical skills, and portrays a gentle bed-side manner. My first doctor's training time spread over a month so she could learn every bit of information from me on how to handle these delicate appointments. In-home pet euthanasia is not easy, no matter what anyone might say. One of my current doctors, an outstanding emergency vet in her own right, struggled to place catheters early on. She found it frustrating that the technique in the home was so different than in the clinic. After a few months, she became much more confident and ready for any kind of patient. I classify my doctors as employees of the company, not independent contractors so that I can maintain more control over techniques and policies and set their schedules.

Conclusion

Exceeding Expectations

As you finish reading this book, I hope you are gaining an appreciation for the high level of care, compassion, and technical skill a euthanasia provider should maintain. You may have learned a few steps you need to take to improve your current practices and reach new standards in animal end-of-life care. Every little detail goes a long way towards showing families and pets how much they mean to you.

Whether you are just starting to consider operating a euthanasia service or have been practicing for years, here are a few ideas that you might adopt to help you exceed your client's expectations and solidify your role as a leader in euthanasia and hospice care within your community:

Before your appointment

- Be supportive and non-judgmental
- Offer families unlimited phone consultations
- Answer your phone 24/7 – or have someone do it for you
- Always return voicemail messages within one hour
- Provide a great website that is informative and calms fears
- If strictly a euthanasia service, still carry a few hospice supplies in case a family is not ready for euthanasia, but their pet needs support
- When providing hospice care, give written information about a pet's disease and what a family might expect as it progresses
- Arrive at the home 5 minutes early
- Be willing to gather ANYWHERE a family chooses in any weather condition
- Be open to helping two pets at once if the family feels it is best for everyone

During the appointment

- Be supportive and non-judgmental
- Look professional and be prepared for anything
- Maintain compassion, confidence, and control
- Learn and use everyone's first names
- Perform a technically strong euthanasia
- Provide a comfortable and attractive blanket for the pet
- Give literature or a book on pet loss and grieving
- Offer private time for the family
- Be willing to show emotion yourself
- Provide a keepsake if the family so desires
- Offer to read a selected poem or prayer if the family is too emotional to do so
- Help the family prepare a grave when necessary
- Guarantee the family at least 1 hour of your time

After the appointment

- Be supportive and non-judgmental
- Notify the pet's veterinarian, groomer, etc.
- Offer a funeral ceremony to honor the pet
- Avoid black garbage bags – offer something nicer when transporting a body
- Personally return the pet's ashes to the family
- Send a sympathy card within 7 days
- Post a pet's name, picture, or a memorial story on your website or in a local paper
- Consider sending a follow-up email 4 weeks later
- Send an anniversary card a year after the pet's death to remind families that they are in your thoughts during this time of remembrance

If we all set the bar high enough, special touches like these will eventually become the norm. Over the coming years, we will see an overwhelming shift towards fully comprehensive geriatric medicine, hospice care, and specialized euthanasia service. Clients will seek out veterinarians trained in end-of-life care as is the case now in human medicine. What an exciting time for our profession.

As you continue on your path, I encourage you to seek continuing educational opportunities in end-of-life care, and if you are having a hard time finding them, request them from national associations and higher learning institutions. Very little is taught about euthanasia in veterinary schools, and private practice is not the best setting to "experiment" and hone your skills. When demand is high enough, lecture series and conferences will be dedicated to this type of work.

A Word from the Author

Since creating the service, Home to Heaven, P.C., in the fall of 2006, I have learned more about humanity, humility, and servitude than I ever dreamed possible. It has been an honor for me to accompany families and pets on their journeys. As you move forward in your work, I hope you feel the same level of professional satisfaction and love that I have.

Be ever mindful to keep your personal life and workload in balance to give you the strength to continue on. Your clients need you. There is no greater feeling than the "Helper's High" this line of work can provide. When you look back over your many years of practice, may you smile and know that you have made a difference.

I want to thank my husband John for giving up his free time so that I could go out on yet another emergency call. For my children, Michael, Shannon, and Jenna, thank you for being so understanding when mommy had to go help the dogs and cats. You deserve a big vacation somewhere soon. To my receptionist Heather, for finding me the time to write and helping to keep everything running smoothly. To my black lab Guber, thank you for being so patient while my doctors "practiced" on you. Thank you to my colleagues who have shared their experiences with me and pushed me to finish the book. And lastly, my sincerest heartfelt thanks to all the families who have welcomed me into their homes over the past 10 years. I am truly honored.

Appendices

Associations Affiliated with End-of-Life Care

American Association of Human-Animal Bond Veterinarians
www.aahabv.org

In-home Pet Euthanasia Directory
www.inhomepeteuthanasia.com

International Veterinary Academy of Pain Management
www.ivapm.org

International Association of Animal Hospice and Palliative Care
www.iaahpc.org

The Association for Pet Loss and Bereavement
www.aplb.org

Compassion Fatigue Scale

Please refer to the included PDF named ProQOL.pdf

For more information on compassion fatitue, I recommend this book:
Compassion Fatigue in the Animal-Care Community, Charles R. Figley and Robert G. Roop, Humane Society Press, 2006

Drug Protocols

Dr. Cooney's protocols as of 2016
(adjusted as needed based on the pet's physical health prior to euthanasia)

Dogs *(use large animal drug concentrations when possible)*

Sedation protocol

Xylazine (100mg/ml) = 0.1 ml per 10#
(also now working a bit more with dexmedetomidine(0.5mg/ml) at 0.1ml per 10# minus 0.1ml. ex. 100# dog would get 0.9ml dexmedetomidine)
Nalbuphine* (20mg/ml) = 0.1 ml per 10#
Acepromazine (10mg/ml) = 0.05 ml per 10#

Anesthesia protocol

Telazol® (100mg/ml) = 0.1 ml per 10#
Xylazine (100mg/ml) = 0.025 ml per 10#
Acepromazine (10mg/ml) = 0.1 ml per 10#
*We use butorphanol when nalbuphine is backordered. Butorphanol (10mg/ml) = 0.1 ml per 10#

Fatal Plus®*

IV, IC = 1 ml per 10# plus 2 mls

IH = 2 mls per 10#

IP = 3 mls per 10#

IR = 6 mls
(cats and exotics only)

*Always check the label for appropriate dosing. AVMA guidelines are similar.

Cats

Anesthesia protocol

Telazol®* (100mg/ml) = 0.1 ml for 2-5#
                           0.2 ml for 5-10#
                           0.3 ml for 10+#
Acepromazine (10mg/ml) = 0.1 ml for all BW

or

Alfaxalone (10mg/ml) = 1.1 -1.5ml for most cats.
Nalbuphine (20mg/ml) = 0.2ml for all BW
Acepromazine (10mg/ml) = 0.1ml for all BW

*Use the same volume of Telazol even if you reconstitute with an opioid or other agent.

Exotics – *guinea pigs, hamsters, chinchillas, rodents, birds, rabbits, reptiles, amphibians, etc*

Telazol® (100mg/ml) = 0.1 ml for <5#
                                0.2 ml for 5-10#
                                0.3 ml for 10+# and all rabbits
Acepromazine (10mg/ml) = 0.1 ml for all BW

For atypical domestic exotics, contact your local specialist for sedation and euthanasia recommendations.

Euthanasia Drugs

Chemical Components and Dosages

Pentobarbital Sodium

Name	Concentration	Class II IV Dose*
Fatal Plus®	390 mg/ml	1 ml/10#
Socumb-6gr®	same	same
Somlethol®	same	same
Sleepaway®	260 mg/ml	2 ml for 1st 10#, then 1 ml per 10

Pentobarbital Sodium with Phenytoin Sodium

Name	Concentration	Class III IV Dose
Beuthanasia-D®	390 mg/ml (pentobarb) 50 mg/ml (phenytoin)	1 ml/10#
Euthasol®	same	same

Pentobarbital Sodium with Lidocaine

Name	Concentration	Class III IV Dose
FP-3®**	390 mg/ml (pentobarb) 20 mg/ml (lidocaine)	1 ml/10#

Kathleen Cooney, D.V.M.

Secobarbitol Sodium with Dibucaine		Class III
Name	**Concentration**	**IV Dose**
Repose®**	400 mg/ml (secobarbitol) 25 mg/ml (dibucaine)	0.22 ml/kg

Embutramide		Class III
Name	**Concentration**	**IV Dose**
T-61®**	200 mg/ml (embutramide) 50 mg/ml (mebozonium iodide) 5 mg/ml (tetracaine HCl)	0.14 ml/lb
Tributame®**	135 mg/ml (embutramide) 35 mg/ml (chloroquine phosphate) 1.9 mg/ml (lidocaine)	1 ml/5#

*Intravenous dosing
**These products are not currently on the market in the U.S.

Potassium Chloride is not listed here as a euthanasia agent for in-home euthanasia. Although approved for use, barbiturate agents are far superior and should be used when available.

Pet Loss Resources

www.petloss.com - families

www.pet-loss.net - families

www.aplb.org - families and vets

www.aspca.org/pet-care/pet-loss - families

http://csuvth.colostate.edu/diagnostic_and_support/argus/ - families, vets

www.veterinarywisdomforpetparents.com - families

www.twoheartspetlosscenter.com/griefguide - vets

Supplies

Drugs, stretchers, body boxes, and euthanasia equipment:
MWI Veterinary Supply, 1-800-824-3703, www.mwivet.com

Clay Paw Prints and related accessories:
World by the Tail, Inc. 1-888-271-8444, www.veterinarywisdom.com

Pet Loss books:
Center for Loss and Life Transition, 970-226-6050, www.centerforloss.com

Andis clippers:
MWI Vet supply or www.andis.com, 1-800-558-9441

Memorial balloons:
www.kathleencooneydvm.com

End-of-life symptoms brochures:
www.kathleencooneydvm.com

Inexpensive body bags:
Four Flags, 1-800-222-9263, www.fourflags.com

World by the Tail, Inc. 1-888-271-8444, www.veterinarywisdom.com

Sympathy cards:
Sole Source, 1-800-285-1657, www.solesource.com

World by the Tail, Inc. 1-888-271-8444, www.veterinarywisdom.com

Business card, brochure, and materials printer (least expensive one I've found):
Got Print, 1-877-922-7374, www.gotprint.com

References

AVMA Guidelines on Euthanasia: Revised 2007

Buddhist view of death, www.eubios.info/EJ144/ej144f.htm

Evans, HE. *Miller's Anatomy of the Dog*. 3rd ed. Philadelphia, PA: W.B. Saunders; 1993

Fakkema, D. *Operational Guide for Animal Care and Control Agencies: Euthanasia by Injection*. American Humane Association; 2010

FDA/Center for Veterinary Medicine, www.fda.gov/animalveterinary/default.htm

Figley, CR, Roop, RG. *Compassion Fatigue in the Animal Care Community*. Washington, D.C.: Humane Society Press; 2006

Fly life cycle, www.buzzle.com/articles/maggots-life-cycle.html

Hanyok, PM. Guidelines for Police Officers When Responding to Emergency Animal Incidents. Animal Welfare Information Center Bulletin, winter 2001/spring 2002, 11(3-4)

Larimer County Burial Guidelines, www.larimer.org/rluc

Mays, J. Euthanasia Certification Powerpoint Presentation. National Animal Control Association, 2010

McMillan, F. Rethinking euthanasia; death as an unintentional outcome. JAVMA 2001 November; Vol 219, No.9. p.1204-06

Pasquini, C, Spurgeon, T. *Anatomy of Domestic Animals*. 5th ed. Pilot Point, TX: Sudz Publishing; 1992

Plumb, DC. *Plumb's Veterinary Drug Handbook*. 5th ed. Ames, IA Blackwell Publishing; 2005

Rhoades, RH. *HSUS Euthanasia Training Manual*, 2002

Rollin, BE. *Animal Rights and Human Morality*, revised edition. Buffalo, NY: Prometheus Books; 1992

Sife, W. *The Loss of a Pet*. 3rd ed. Hoboken, NJ: Wiley Publishing; 2005

USFWS Fact Sheet on Secondary Pentobarbital Poisoning In Wildlife, http://cpharm.vetmed.vt.edu/USFWS/

Villalobos, A. *Canine and Feline Geriatric Oncology. Honoring the Human-Animal Bond*. Blackwell Publishing, Table 10.1, released 2006

Wadham, JB. Intraperitoneal injection of sodium pentobarbitone as a method of euthanasia for rodents. ANZCCART News 1997;10(4):8

Wolfelt, A. *When Your Pet Dies: A guide to mourning, remembering, and healing*. Companion Press. 2004

WSPA Methods for the Euthanasia of Dogs and Cats; Comparison and Recommendations. Online PDF publication London, England www.ebookbrowse.com/euthanasia-methods-pdf-d73621029

Pet Loss Memorial Readings: www.belovedcommunitypetministry.com

www.ingramcontent.com/pod-product-compliance
Lightning Source LLC
Chambersburg PA
CBHW042056290426
44111CB00001B/22